WATERSIDE WALKING IN THE PEAK DISTRICT

WATERSIDE WALKING IN THE PEAK DISTRICT

Keith Stevens

Published by Sigma Leisure – an imprint of
Sigma Press, Stobart House, Pontyclerc, Penybanc Road, Ammanford, Carmarthenshire SA18 3HP.

British Library Cataloguing in Publication Data
A CIP record for this book is available from the British Library.

ISBN: 978-1-85058-936-5

Typesetting and Design by: Sigma Press, Ammanford.

Cover photograph: © Keith Stevens, Macclesfield Forest across Bottoms Reservoir

Maps, drawings and photographs: © Keith Stevens

Route sketch maker: Peter Whittaker

Printed by: TJ International Ltd, Padstow, Cornwall

Disclaimer: The information in this book is given in good faith and is believed to be correct at the time of publication. No responsibility is accepted by either the author or publisher for errors or omissions, or for any loss or injury howsoever caused. Only you can judge your own fitness, competence and experience. Do not rely solely on the sketch maps to navigate, we strongly recommend the use of appropriate Ordnance Survey (or equivalent) maps.

Preface

Water – we take it for granted. We enjoy it, sailing, skiing and swimming, but we also waste it and pollute it. One day, the lack of fresh water could be the greatest 'doom and gloom' scenario to sweep the planet, dwarfing even global warming and colliding asteroids. In the meantime, we might as well enjoy it. And what better way than with a refreshing family walk, witnessing water in all its natural beauty, be it the tumbling magnificence of a mountain stream or the manmade landscape of canals and reservoirs.

The Derbyshire Peaks are crossed by a score of splendid rivers, each telling its own story, with fabulous walking. Surprisingly, there are over 50 reservoirs, many offering stunning scenery and great walking. And there are the canals, with their long history and their working and leisure cultures. So finding 30 superb waterside walks was easy.

Each walk has a route map, but an OS map to hand is always a good idea, and is helpful when reading the account about the rivers. For most of the walks, five or six miles (10 km) is the limit, with modest gradients and generally easy terrain. They are walks that can be enjoyed by all age groups, from six to sixty and beyond, and none are in the strenuous category.

The walks ar situated within the Derbyshire Peaks, between Congleton and Matlock and from Ashbourne to Holmfirth, keeping to rights of way alongside or near the water, and avoiding difficult areas such as bleak peat moorland. They are all circular, so that the whole walk cannot be by the water – few people like 'there and back' walks; there has to be a return route. The narrative also provides information on where to start, how to get there from the nearest town and on the walk length and height gain.

Finally, and most importantly, there is plenty to see and learn, with fascinating information about how the water systems work, the history and the geology, and surrounding countryside and local culture. How is our drinking water managed? Where do the rivers begin, and where do they end up? How are the canals topped up? Why do some rivers suddenly disappear? What made the old mills work? It's all answered here.

There's something in it for everyone – parents, grandparents and children alike. Get the kids out into the fresh air, away from the computer, enjoy the scenery, face a few challenges – they'll enjoy it.

Contents

Reservoir key

1. Butterley, Blakely, Wessenden and Wessenden Head to the east, in a line. Brunclough, Redbrook, Swellands, Black Moss, Little Black Moss (too small to show) and Diggle in a cluster to the west.
2. Greenfield, Yeoman Hey, Dove Stone and Chew, all linked.
3. Digley and Bilberry to the north, and Ramsden, Riding Wood and Yateholme in a group below. Brownhill Reservoir is nearby, just outside the Peak District boundary.
4. Snailsden, Harden and Windscar to the north, with two Windelden reservoirs below. (There are no sensible walks around any of these.)
5. Bottoms, Valehouse, Rhodeswood, Torside and Woodhead in a line.
6. Langsett Reservoir, with Midhope just outside the boundary.
7. Broomhead Reservoir, with More Hall Reservoir just outside the boundary. (Too wooded for a good waterside walk.)
8. Howden, Derwent and Ladybower, all linked.
9. Strines, Dale Dike, Agden and Damflask, around Low Bradfield.
10. Kinder Reservoir.
11. Three Redmires reservoirs to the south, with two Rivelin Dams above.
12. Horse Coppice and Bollinhurst in Lyme Park, on the boundary.
13. Barbrook Reservoir (breached, downgraded by EU regulations).
14. Fernilee and Errwood, with Lamaload to the west.
15. Longstone Reservoir.
16. Trentabank, with Ridgegate, Bottoms and Teggsnose reservoirs just outside the boundary.
17. Tittersworth on the boundary, and Rudyard just outside.
18. The very large Carsington Water, three miles outside the boundary.

There are also four small reservoirs (Hurst, Mossy Lea, Swineshaw and Upper Swineshaw) near Glossop, a few more only just outside the boundary (for instance, Combs, near Chapel-en-le-Frith), and it's always possible that I missed the odd small one. Surprisingly, could find very few natural lakes or pools – they all seem to be manmade. The biggest I came across was the very modest 'Turner's Pool', just west of the Roaches, and the pool on Bleakley Dike, SE of Youlgreave. There's also a small lake in Lyme Park Country Park near Macclesfield, as well as the two reservoirs.

Water in The Peak District

At least 50 reservoirs and about 20 major rivers; that was my count after scouring the OS maps. I've tried to fit them on the map below, with details of the reservoir names on the opposite page.

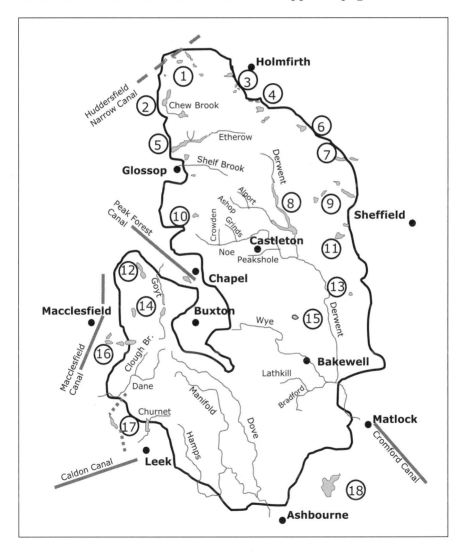

The rivers

In the north of the Peak District, the moorland is drained by a plethora of cloughs and streams, with only Chew Brook presenting a decent opportunity for adjacent walking. I've included that one with a walk around the nearby reservoirs.

Coming south to Crowden on the north side of Torside Reservoir, there are two major streams that converge, Crowden Great Brook (with the Pennine Way alongside) and Crowden Little Brook. They would make a splendid circular walk if only you didn't have to wade across Siddens Moss at the top. I abandoned that idea for a family outing. And the main river that feeds the Torside Reservoir group, the Etherow, follows the A628, so presents few opportunities.

The source of the Derwent is on Howden Moor, north of the three reservoirs, Howden, Derwent and Ladybower. There's a path along it, and in the past I've done a circular walk that included Howden Moor. Once was enough! However, the southern stretches of the Derwent, on its way to the Trent via Hathersage, Nether Padley and Matlock, provide a number of excellent walking areas.

The Derwent is joined by the Noe, a river that rises at Edale Head and follows the Pennine Way by Jacobs Ladder. It has two main tributaries coming off the Kinder plateau, Grinds Brook and Crowden Great Brook (same name as above). Between them, there are some fabulous waterside walks, but all too strenuous for this book. Finally, the Noe is joined by Peakshole Water, originating from the Great Ridge via Castleton. Although Castleton and Hope are very popular, there were no waterside walks on the Noe or Peakshole that I was happy with.

Ladybower is also fed by the River Ashop, rising off Ashop Moor under the north face of Kinder. It's accompanied by the Snake Path, but any circular walk is strenuous. Then it follows the A57, which is not helpful. But its tributary, the Alport (rising at Alport Head on Bleaklow moor), presents a splendid walk that takes in the Alport Castles rock formations. Alas, it is too strenuous for inclusion in this book. I've also drawn in Shelf Brook on the map, leaving Bleaklow westwards through Glossop, eventually joining the Etherow. The walk along Doctor's Gate is very popular, but if you wanted a circular route you'd have to be prepared for ten miles of hard slog.

To the east, the River Don is outside the Peak District, but fed by rivers coming off the high ground around several of the reservoirs. One is the Loxley, featured in the walks around the Low Bradfield reservoirs.

To the west, the Goyt, both before and after the Fernilee and Errwood reservoirs, is very picturesque, with two good walks that include the reservoirs. It rises from the area around the Cat and Fiddle pub and eventually joins the Etherow on its way to the Mersey. Then the Dane rises on the other side of the Cat and Fiddle ridge, from Axe Edge Moor, flowing through Congleton and out to the Weaver and Mersey. There are a couple of decent walks on the Dane, and it's joined by Clough Brook (through Wildboarclough, rising west of the Cat and Fiddle), another pleasant walking area. South of the Dane, the Churnet presents few walking opportunities, but it does supply Tittersworth Reservoir, which features in one of the walks.

Finally, around Buxton and Bakewell, the Wye provides for splendid walking opportunities, with its gorges and disused railway. It runs into the Derwent, joined on its way by the Lathkill and the Bradford, both running through stunning valleys. Then south, the limestone rivers are the Dove (from Axe Edge) and the Manifold (from Flash), joined by the Hamps (off Merryton Low near the Mermaid pub), eventually running into the Trent. Between them, they rate some of the best walks in the Peak District. However, because the Hamps is nearly always dry, I have not included it in this selection.

The canals

As far as I can see, there aren't any canals within the Peak District boundary, unless you count the Huddersfield Narrow Canal that runs underneath, through a tunnel near Diggle (dotted line on the map, NW corner). There are several just outside the boundary, and they are important to the theme of this book, involving some of the reservoirs. Although just outside the National Park boundary, I've included a walk taking in part of the Peak Forest Canal.

As well as the five canals that are named on the map, there are two man-made channels running from (a 'leat') and into (a 'conduit') Rudyard Reservoir (No 17 on the water map), depicted by short dotted lines. They are both discussed during the walk narratives. A conduit walk also forms part of the route round the Redmires reservoirs.

The walks

The 30 walks are grouped by region to help you plan your journeys. For each one I've indicated the start and parking facilities, the route and its degree of difficulty, including the distance, total ascent, climbing gradient and estimated walking time. That is based on an

The walks and their locations

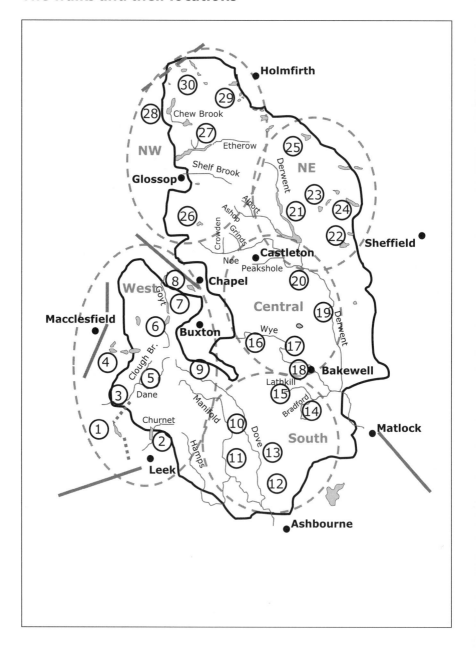

No.	Area visited	No.	Area visited
1	Rudyard Reservoir	16	Miller's Dale and Chee Dale, on the River Wye
2	Tittersworth Reservoir	17	Monasal Dale and Litton Mill, on the River Wye
3	The Rudyard Conduit and the River Dane	18	Monsal Dale and Ashford, on the River Wye
4	Macclesfield Forest and Four Reservoirs	19	River Derwent and Froggatt Edge
5	Three Shires and Three Rivers	20	River Derwent – Shatton to Leadmill
6	Errwood Reservoir	21	Derwent Reservoir
7	Fernilee Reservoir and Windgather Rocks	22	Rivelin and Redmires Reservoirs
8	Peak Forest Canal and Eccles Pike	23	Dale Dike and Strines Reservoirs
9	River Dove and High Wheeldon	24	Agden and Damflask Reservoirs
10	River Manifold – Wettonmill and Ecton	25	Langsett Reservoir
11	River Manifold and Thor's cave	26	Kinder Reservoir
12	Ilam and Dove Dale	27	Torside Reservoir
13	Biggin Dale and Wolfscote Dale, on the River Dove	28	Dove Stone, Greenfield and Yeoman Hey Reservoirs
14	Bradford Dale and Youlgreave	29	Holmbridge – Six Reservoirs
15	Lathkill Dale and Over Haddon	30	Marsden – Six Reservoirs

average speed of about 3 km/hour (2 miles/hour) to allow extra time for rest and observation. In some cases there are optional shorter routes, with special consideration for the children. Wherever possible, I've designed the walk route to give a view of the water feature from higher ground, in addition to the section that is alongside the water itself.

All the walks are on established rights of way, open-access areas and accepted concessionary paths. There is some road walking, mostly on quiet lanes. There's a route sketch, good enough for you to follow the walk, but the relevant OS map will help if you want to review the wider picture about the various water features. In the interests of the water theme, and in providing good walks, some routes are just outside the official Peak District National Park boundary.

Concerning safety, it's obvious that any walk might present hazards, but most of the routes in this book will suit the whole family, with children as young as six. If there are any particular hazards I discuss them in the walk summary and during the narrative, and I explain that some of the longer walks are best suited for families with older children.

Distances are primarily in kilometres and metres, but there are conversions to miles to help. For short distances, a metre and a yard can be considered equivalent. Elevations are in metres, with conversion to feet.

Finally, I did not reconnoitre the walks in the order as presented in the book, so that in a year when rainfall was so varied (2010), the discussion about reservoir and river levels does not tell a continuous story.

Walk 1 – Rudyard Reservoir

Around the reservoir, south on the east side, going beyond the dam to look at the miniature trains, and returning north on the west side. The car park by the dam costs money, and it's useful to have the male orientated attraction of the steam engines in the middle of the walk, rather than too early.

Distance and climb	**8.5 km (5.3 miles) and 130m (450 ft), taking about 2.5 hours**
Grading	**Easy, climbing gradient 1 in 18, children friendly**
OS map	**Landranger 118**
Start	**Reacliffe Road, north end of Rudyard Reservoir** **From the A623 Macclesfield/Leek road, take Beat Lane westwards from Rycroft Gate, 1.5 km (one mile) south of Rushton Spencer. After 200m, before the stream bridge, go left (south) along Reacliffe Road. Parking is then after 500m. It's potholed – 5 mph is advised. My VW Golf coped with ease, and it's worth it to start at the north of the reservoir.**

The walk

From the car, walk south, keeping left under the bridge, and follow the old railway track. The disused line joined North Rode with Leek as part of the Churnet Valley Railway, and it hasn't seen a real train since 1964.

A magical engine

The first views of the reservoir come after 400m, and 100m further on there is a line of crumbling posts; remnants of the old railway. The route follows the track all the way to the dam, with the miniature railway alongside, and you might see Merlin or one of the other engines in action, each with a name in keeping with a 'King Arthur' theme.

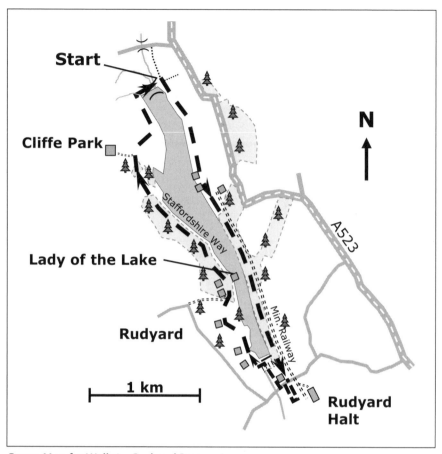

Route Map for Walk 1 – Rudyard Reservoir

On the way, enjoy the views across the reservoir to the elegant properties on the west bank, and look for a boathouse that protrudes into the water. There's a woman clinging to the chimney – 'The Lady of the Lake' – you might need your binoculars to best appreciate her attributes.

With the dam in sight 300m away, you could take the steps on the right to gain a higher vantage point. There are some picnic tables if you fancy a break to view the boats, then the path leads back down to the dam.

Don't cross the dam there; carry on south, over the road bridge to the terminus, Rudyard Halt. Apparently, the miniature railway was laid single-handedly by one man, Peter Hampton, finishing in 1985. There are four steam engines, as well as a diesel and a petrol version - so there's no shortage of pulling power.

Having had a look around, walk down to the lane and turn left. Then it's 50m, past the garage, to a metal walker's gate on the right. Take that and follow the leat back to the dam. It's a manmade channel that carries water from the reservoir to the start of the Caldon Canal 5 km (three miles) away at Barnfields, SW of Leek. So, like several others in the Peak District, Rudyard is not storing drinking water; it's a header reservoir for the canal, built in 1797.

The map shows how it works. The leat feeds the head of the canal, so when boats travel through the locks, taking slugs of water with them, the water level is replenished.

Although the canal follows the River Churnet for much of its route, it's not possible to use the river as a source of water. The canal is deliberately about 8m (25 ft) higher than the river, and it's easy to see that, if the canal had been built on the same level, any flooding by the river in wet weather would overwhelm the

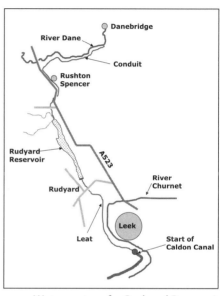

Water system for Rudyard Reservoir

canal. In fact, the river is used as an outlet for any excess water in the canal, a principle adopted for all canals.

Looking to the north end of the reservoir, as well as two natural streams, it is fed by another manmade channel, called a conduit, which takes water off the River Dane just south of Danebridge. So the Caldon Canal is partially topped up by the River Dane from about 11 km (seven miles) away. (The conduit features in Walk 3.)

Just before the dam there is a complex series of leats designed to manage the water. If too much volume is coming through the dam spillway, threatening to overwhelm the canal, excess water is taken off over the weirs to flood the marsh to the south of the dam wall. And, later in its route, the leat has several sluice outlets that can allow more water to run off into the Churnet if needed.

At the foot of the dam, go right up the diagonal path to the top, where you can enjoy some seats and a good view down the reservoir, with its boats and expensive villas. There's also an information board with interesting facts about the area.

What came first, the reservoir or the poet? It was the reservoir - with the village probably named after a landowner many centuries ago, 'Rudyard' being a male given name meaning 'red' and 'reserved'. Then Rudyard Kipling the poet got his name after his parents had visited the reservoir and fallen in love with it in 1863.

On the west side of the dam there's a visitor's centre - it's well worth a look, with interesting detail on the reservoir and the wildlife. From there, walk by the water, around the hotel, taking the path to the left up to Lake Road at the top. Go right there; then keep left up the track (not into 'The Crescent', which is a dead end). It's the Staffordshire Way, with the 'knot' signs to guide you, and with properties to the right. It becomes a walled track and joins a tarmac access road where you go right, downhill, back towards the water.

Reservoir view

At the gate to the property called 'Belmont', go left though the wooded area, eventually emerging on to a lane, where you turn right, following the edge of the reservoir for the rest of the walk. You'll pass by a gate with the name 'Fortside' on it (written in Old English style, referring to a bungalow on the waterfront). So where's the fort? There never was one – back in the 1920s, the owner of the Lady of the Lake property called it his 'fort'. This was because he could barricade the causeway to keep his wife at bay whilst he entertained his mistress! (Apocryphal.)

Continuing on, it's pleasant walking through the trees. You'll pass a derelict castellated building – it was the lodge to Cliffe Park Hall, where the underlings lived, and from there to the hall itself was known as Lovers Walk. Inevitably, the hall was built by a rich silk manufacturer, probably with money earned from the sweat of his downtrodden mill girls (in 1911). Since then it's been a golf clubhouse, a youth hostel and now a private residence. It looks a good bet for flat conversions to me.

From the hall, take the gate at the cattle grid and follow the track down to the lane and back towards the water. Finally, as you approach the parking spot, you'll pass over the conduit feeding the reservoir, the subject of Walk 3.

Walk 2 – Tittersworth Reservoir

Clockwise around the reservoir, following the path that keeps closest to the water, with some lane walking on the return side. There's a Visitor Centre, picnic areas and extensive adventure and play facilities for the children. You can get a pushchair around this route, with some steps to negotiate, and I think it's one of the best family walks I've come across. It's also dog friendly.

There's a parking charge, so I stopped on the lane side east of the reservoir (towards Middle Hulme), where the parking restrictions ended. In busy times, that opportunity might be limited.

Distance and climb	7.2 km (4.5 miles) and 125m (400 ft), taking about 2.5 hours
Grading	Easy, climbing gradient 1 in 13, children friendly
OS map	Landranger 118
Start	Visitor's car park at the reservoir, or from the lane east of the reservoir Go 1.5 km (one mile) west on the lane that leaves the A53 Buxton/Leek road by the Three Horseshoes pub, 3 km (two miles) NE of Leek. Or SE by the lanes from Ruston Spencer (on the A523 Macclesfield/Leek road), following the signs for Meerbrook.

The walk

Severn Trent Water has certainly put itself out, with excellent catering for the walking family. I wonder if they make a profit out of it? The Visitor Centre is worth looking into, with information boards about the reservoir, its history, how the water is managed, the wildlife, and the walks. I've followed 'The Long Walk', which you will see described and sign-

The Roaches and Hen Cloud

posted, so there is no need here for a lot of narrative. There's a well-made limestone path all the way to the dam, but whenever possible I took the grassy path detours that kept close to the water's edge.

Starting from the Visitor Centre parking area, go east, passing the adventure playground and a formidable wooden seat (if it's still there), and follow the path around Churnet Bay, which is the primary feed for the

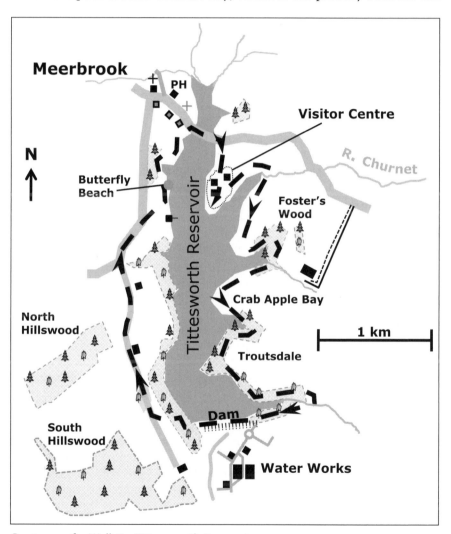

Route map for Walk 2 – Tittersworth Reservoir

reservoir. To the east is an excellent view of The Roaches, with the distinctive Hen Cloud outcrop at the southern end. Further SE, 5 km away (three miles), in a dip in the hills that make the horizon, is 'The Mermaid' pub near Merryton Low.

Keep right as you go around the inlet, cross two bridges, and then leave the main track to take the grassy path at the 'Q' marker post. There's meadow, the water and Foster's Wood, and it was from the water's edge there that I got my best pictures of The Roaches. And across the reservoir to the west is a good view of the gentle Gun Hill.

It's pleasant walking through the wood, rejoining the main track, looping around the inlet and then taking to the grass again at the marker post showing 'To Haregate'. This one directs you along the Crab Apple Bay inlet, in the wood of the same name, crossing a stream, climbing the steps and returning to the track at the top.

Walking on, the track then circles the Troutsdale inlet, and it was on this leg that I met a large party of very senior citizens. The humorous 'whipper in' at the back told me that, if he started with such a group of 30, and got back with 28 or 29, he was happy. That small level of 'wastage' was considered acceptable, he said! Perhaps, one day, that will be my fate.

The track leads round to the dam (on the way, ignore the path to Haregate that leaves left by a walker's gate), and you get your first view of how it all works. There is the overspill for wet weather, and looking south, below you, there is the outlet for the ongoing River Churnet. Then over to the left is the treatment facility, where the reservoir water is purified to drinking standards and sent on to more, closed, storage reservoirs nearer the users.

The main input of water to the reservoir is from the River Churnet at the NE corner, added to by numerous smaller incoming streams around the perimeter. The output is the river below the dam face and an unseen amount going through the treatment works. It means that the ongoing River Churnet must be a shadow of its former self, pre-reservoir days (1858). But, by way of compensation, it probably gets a lot of the water back downstream, after it's been 'processed' by the good people of the Potteries. And the reservoir name? 'Worth' means 'enclosure', so the origin will be many hundreds of years old – an enclosure for animals owned by a man with a name similar to 'Titters'.

From the dam centre I tried an innovative panoramic view of the reservoir by linking a sequence of photographs, which is how the image comes to show the parapet leading away in two directions. It works OK, but some rowing boats or kayaks would have been nice on such a

Tittersworth Reservoir from the centre of the dam

beautiful day. It was early spring 2010, and the reservoir was nearly full, the coming drought not yet having taken its toll.

From the dam, take the steps on the west side. There's a pillar at the start – it's a survey point for the dam, used to look for any movements or changes in levels. (The height above sea level of the top of the pillar will be very precisely known.) At the top you emerge into pasture, where you go right on the hard lane. There, I spotted a woodpecker in a tree above my head. I froze. He hammered, looked down at me, then hammered some more. But as soon as I made the slightest move to raise my camera, he was off. Most annoying – I've always wanted such a picture.

On this stretch, the views east have expanded, so you can now see Ramshaw Rocks (behind Hen Cloud to the right). Then the track leads through South Hillswood Farm and to a lane over a cattle grid, where you go right. After 300m, go right again, down the track to 'Peak Pursuits'. It's a leisure organisation, including boat hire. No engine-driven craft are allowed; only non-polluting canoes and kayaks. If you're not tempted, go left as the track reaches the water, and pass by the interesting 'Butterfly Beach', a commendable initiative to encourage the wildlife. I saw none, but I was there early in the year.

From there the path takes you across a stream and back to the lane, where you turn right across the water and to the car. There are good views down the reservoir from there, but photographs looking towards the sun never seem to work for me. There's also a nature reserve to the north, including an island, which you can explore if you still have some walking energy left.

Walk 3 – The Rudyard Conduit and the River Dane

NW along the disused railway to intercept 'The Dane Valley Way', then following the Conduit to its junction with the River Dane. Return is via the Dane, a track through Whitelee Farm and 'The Gritstone Trail', crossing the outward route to make a figure of eight shaped walk. An optional shortcut is indicated, reducing the distance to 8 km (five miles).

Distance and climb	9.8 km (6.1 miles) and 200m (650 ft), taking about three hours
Grading	Easy, climbing gradient 1 in 14, children friendly
OS map	Landranger 118
Start	Rushton Spencer is 11 km (seven miles) south of Macclesfield on the A523 Leek Road. From the village, take Station Road westward for 200m and turn left after 'The Knot' pub to the walker's car park by the disused railway. Or you can park roadside on Station Road.

The walk

From Station Road, follow the disused railway NW. It's the same Churnet Valley Railway described in Walk 1 by Rudyard Reservoir, joining North Rode with Leek. It's pleasant walking with views either side, and it's 1 km (half a mile) to the bridge that is the limit of walker's access.

Drop down to the meadow and turn right under the bridge, following the signpost indicating 'Gritstone Trail - Lyme Park.' The path crosses the main road and follows the edge of a cultivated field to a stile, with the River Dane to the left and the conduit on the higher ground to the right. After the stile, turn diagonally right and walk up to the bridge that spans the conduit. Then take the gate on the left and follow the path alongside the channel (Gritstone Trail and Dane Valley Way).

It's clear at this point that the conduit is higher than the Dane, but that they must eventually come together at the same elevation. That point is still 3 km (two miles) away, and the walk by the channel is easy and interesting. I did it in June 2010 when a hosepipe ban was being muted,

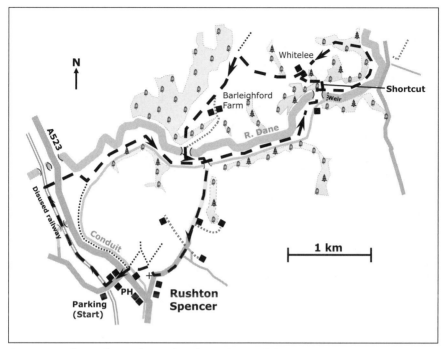

Route Map for Walk 3 – The Rudyard Conduit and the River Dane

so I was surprised to see that the conduit was quite full, even though it was overgrown in places. But I could detect no discernible flow.

1.5 km (one mile) on, the path reaches a track crossing the conduit over a bridge. It comes up from the river (The Gritstone Trail) and it's the return leg of the walk, crossing the outward path. Continue along the conduit from that point, with the river steadily rising closer to your level. Within 100m you cross an overflow, coming off the conduit and running down the slope towards the Dane, taking away excess water during extreme weather.

As the conduit turns north, with the river close by and getting higher, there is a property (Hammond's Hole) and what looks like a nature reserve, with piles of logs and stones. A good place for snakes, I'd say. The conduit has been widened there, so that ducks were quacking and I was privileged to glimpse a Kingfisher. Reading a book on the history of the Dane, I've seen a picture of two Edwardian ladies in a small boat, with the conduit looking wider and deeper than today (reprinted below). I suspect it was taken at that spot.

Weir header for the conduit

Near the end of the conduit, the embankment on which you're walking gets higher, ensuring that the river and the conduit are securely separated. Next is the Dane, with a metal bridge overlooking the weir. I found it intimidating, but then I'm a wimp. To put that in perspective, looking at the old pictures again, this time the two Edwardian Ladies are edging across a rope bridge – a forerunner of the present bridge. There is absolutely no way I could have done that.

Re-printed by kind permission of the publishers and authors of 'The Dane Valley Way' by Mary and Colin McLean, S B Publications Ltd

The two diagrams show how the conduit was managed. At 'A' (the weir), the Dane and the conduit are at the same height above sea level. As they separate, the Dane flows on towards Congleton, falling with a gradient of 1 in 100 up to and beyond point 'G'. In contrast, the conduit falls very slowly over the equivalent distance, dropping only 9m (28 ft) in 4 km (two and a half miles) before it reaches Rudyard Reservoir; a gradient of 1 in 700. So its flow rate was always pedestrian, delivering a small but steady volume of water from the Dane to the reservoir.

How much water went down the Conduit? It's hard to say, because the demand from the reservoir is now relatively low. One hundred years ago, with massive coal

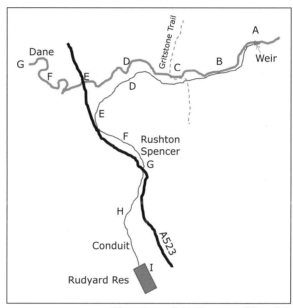

Plan view of the Dane and Conduit

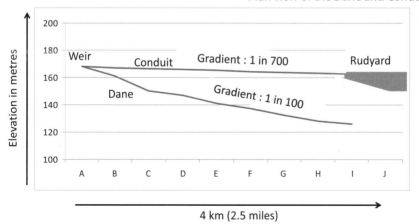

Gradients of the Dane and the Conduit

barges going down the locks on the Caldon Canal, Rudyard would have been hard-pushed to keep up with the supply. If the reservoir level dropped, even by 2m, it would add greatly to the gradient at the end of the conduit, and the flow would significantly increase. Then it would be a question of taking enough water from the top of the weir on the Dane to keep up, controlled, I think, by a sluice.

On the other side of the Dane bridge, my route goes right, by the river. But there is a shortcut at that point, if you are so minded, up the slope alongside the trees towards a field track. Then look for where the path turns left through the trees, continuing up the hill on the other side, with the trees now on the right, emerging by Whitelee Farm.

The longer route takes you through pleasant meadows, with more weirs to enjoy, turning north as the river loops away from the path. Where it loops back again, look for a field gate into the trees on the left, leading to a steep path up to a metalled track, where you go left. That track emerges into open countryside, with a good view SE to The Roaches, and leads through Whitelee Farm, emerging on to a drive on the other side, where the shortcut route comes up from below. At the farm they'd gone out of their way to entertain the walkers with some curious model animals – it's nice to see.

Hairy pigs

The drive becomes a track and leads to a field gate to open pasture, where the path is vague. Carry straight on, but veer a little right, with a fence eventually joining your left flank, and with views to the fore to The Cloud and the long sweep of Bosley Minn. There's a stile, then another as you intercept the Gritstone Way, where you turn left.

More pleasant walking follows, with the wooded Shell Brook valley to the right, the route leading around Barleighford Farm (avoid following the fence to the back for the farm – keep right) and down to the Dane. On the other side you cross the outgoing route alongside the conduit and follow the metalled track back towards Ruston Spencer. It becomes a lane, crosses a stream, joins another lane from the left and then goes downhill, with a chapel at the bottom.

To avoid walking along the main road, just before the corner with the chapel, take the public footpath to the right, between the hedges. It leads through a kissing gate, down some steps and emerges into a managed area, with a stream. Keep left and cross the wide footbridge, with a gate marked 'Private' then to the fore. Veer left again there, over a stile, and then keep straight on to cross back over the stream on a second footbridge. There's another stile, before the path leads rather intrusively through a property and along a metalled track, crossing the stream yet again, as well as the conduit, and joining Tanhouse Lane. Then all you have to do is cross the main road back into Station Road.

Walk 4 – Macclesfield Forest and Four Reservoirs

First, a look at Trentabank Reservoir, then west by Ridgegate Reservoir and on to the Bottoms and Teggsnose reservoirs via the Gritstone Trail. The short route keeps below Tegg's Nose, on the way to Hardingland. The longer route takes in the summit. Return is via the forest tracks and the lanes past the Leather's Smithy pub. Tegg's Nose summit is a stiff climb, but there is plenty to see, with good views of the reservoirs.

Distance and climb	**7.4 km (4.6 miles) and 220m (730 ft), taking 2.5 hours, or 9 km (5.6 miles) and 340m (1,100 ft) if Tegg's Nose summit is visited, taking three hours**
Grading	**Easy, climbing gradient 1 in 12, children friendly. Moderate, with a climbing gradient of 1 in 10, if including Tegg's Nose**
OS map	**Landranger 118**
Start	**Walker's car park in Macclesfield Forest. From Macclesfield, take Byrons Lane to Sutton and Langley. From Langley, drive east uphill, past Bottoms Reservoir, and turn right at the Leather's Smithy pub, alongside Ridgegate Reservoir. The car park and Ranger's Headquarters are then 1 km (0.6 mile). Parking roadside is usually possible, to avoid the charges**

The walk

From the car park, cross the lane and go east (right) a little to find a walker's gate and a path to a viewing point over Trentabank Reservoir. There's another on the roadside 300m further to the east. It's as close as you can get, since the area is a nature reserve and Heronry. There're some useful notice boards, and leaflets at the Ranger Station give information

Trentabank Reservoir at low ebb

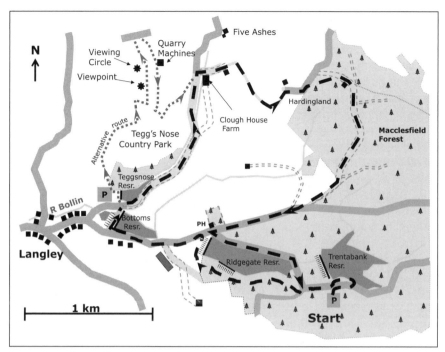

Route Map for Walk 4 – Macclesfield Forest and Four Reservoirs

about the wildlife, including the elusive red deer. (I've never seen one.)

The nature reserve means that Trentabank Reservoir is mostly out of bounds, so that a circular walk coming back on its eastern edge is difficult. But I got a good photo, at a time of drought (June 2010), with old tracks and gateposts emerging from the depths.

To start the walk proper, go back west along the lane, down to the right-hand bend, and take the wall stile on to the bridle track opposite. Go left (not right, as might be assumed), following the track across a stream and through the wooded area on the southern flank of Ridgegate Reservoir. The outlook across the water unfolds,

Tegg's Nose across Ridgegate Reservoir

and eventually there is a nice view to the Tegg's Nose hill, with the Leather's Smithy pub in the foreground. In June 2010 the water was very low, but the fisherman was enjoying his best catch in years.

Ridgegate has two dams, so that you traverse one on the south side, with the outlet for the water at the bottom and overspill channel at the west end. Then the path veers left through the trees and emerges into a clearing, approaching the second dam at the western end. Here, the view to the fore is of Tegg's Nose, with the ridge from Ward's Knob leading up from the west, your onward route if you intend visiting the summit.

Following the fingerpost to Langley, walk below the western dam and emerge on to Clarke Lane by the pub, turning left there and going downhill. You'll pass the Ridgegate Water Treatment facility on the left; then you get the first view of Bottoms Reservoir on the right. Mine was delightful, with the water covered in colourful lilies and a Great Crested Grebe nesting on the surface, its mate stood nearby, preening itself.

As you reach a row of cottages, take the gate on the right and follow the Gritstone Trail across

The nest must be a raft

the Bottoms dam, with the chance of a good picture back towards the forest.

With Teggsnose Reservoir to come, that's four in total. So what are they for? The diagram below shows how it works, with Ridgegate and Trentabank supplying water to Macclesfield and the surrounding area. They take their water from the forest catchment, including the Bollin Brook, so it's possible that the onward River Bollin (meaning 'River from the rounded hill') would be depleted during dry summer spells. That would hardly have done for the rich mill owners downstream (Styal and Quarry Bank, for instance), since they relied on the turning mill wheels to make them even richer. So that is what Bottoms and Teggsnose were for, creating a header to keep the river flowing on its way to the Mersey.

Ridgegate was built first (in 1850), cutting off the main supply to the Bollin, with Bottoms built at the same time to keep a head for the river, mainly from water coming down Hardingland Brook. Presumably, that was not good enough for the powerful mill lobby, because Teggsnose

Macclesfield Forest across Bottoms Reservoir

Reservoir followed in 1871, collecting water from Walker Barn Brook as an extra cushion. Trentabank came later (1920) as additional storage, essentially an extension to Ridgegate.

At the end of the Bottoms dam, before crossing the bridge over the overspill channel, make an excursion down the steps to look at the valve house. It controls the flow into a small pool (about 6m lower than the reservoir) that forms the start of the river. I think it's a way of assessing the required output from the reservoirs – keep that pool at a certain level and all will be well.

Walking on over the footbridge and up the steps to the gate, the short walk turns right along the track ('Public Bridleway – no vehicles') on the SE side of Teggsnose Reservoir. If you are going to visit the summit, then walk left instead on the Gritstone Trail, along the Teggsnose dam to the parking area at the other end. Then turn to the final part of this walk narrative to follow the route over the top, before coming back to paragraph * below.

* The short route track skirts Tegg's Nose forest, fords the Walker Barn Brook and emerges (after 1.5 km – a mile – and via a couple of gates) on

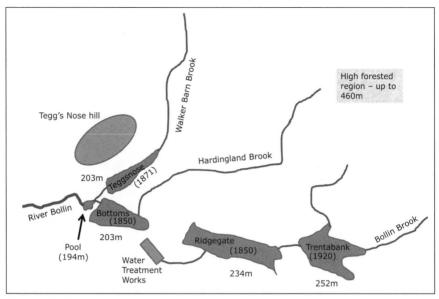

Reservoir plan

to the sharp corner of a lane. Go right there, steeply downhill, past Clough House Farm, and up the other side. The lane reaches Lower Crooked Yard Farm before it becomes a narrow track. The property name implies that there is a higher version somewhere nearby and, bizarrely, that two farms in close proximity both have yards that are crooked. Can't see it myself!

The track turns right, fords a stream and rises steeply on the other side. I've walked that track when it was doubling up as a river, but in June 2010 there was nothing but dust. At the top, the track turns left (with good views behind at that point – always look back now and again) and reaches the lane at Hardingland Farm, where you walk on for 150m and take the gate on to the forest track.

At the next fingerpost, keep right towards Forest Chapel and you will soon encounter a derelict stone building, beyond which the path reaches a wide forest track. Go right, following it downhill (a track also joins from the left just there). It's a pleasant descent (called the Forest Bridleway), with views in front to the BT tower on Croker Hill, and the track eventually reaches a gate on to Clarke Lane. From there to the pub is 1 km (half a mile), where you turn left alongside Ridgegate on your way back to the car. In June 2010, the flies were buzzing and dozens of fish were jumping. No wonder the angler in my first photograph was having a good day.

Longer route – the excursion over Tegg's Nose summit

Entry to the country park is on the left of the small car park, through a wrought iron gate. The path follows a steep flight of steps, passing through a wooded area and emerging into open grassland. At the top, after a short set of stone steps, a gate marks the entrance to the track that circles the Tegg's Nose summit. Turn left there, walk 200m to the next gate, turn back right along the track for 100m and finally turn left again just before the next gate. That path leads up to a vantage point, with a 'Skylark's View' information board describing the panoramic landscape to the west.

From that viewing point, walk uphill again in a northerly direction to another unusual feature. It's a stone-walled circle with a series of spy-ports, each with a name describing the feature that can be seen in the distance. Whilst at the walled circle, look over the quarry edge to the east for a good view of some quarrying machines set out below, superbly preserved from a bygone age. The area below is actually on the

Quarry machinery

return path, but the route first continues north for 400m, keeping to the top of the ridge, before dropping down on to the track at the end. There, turn back south, passing by the machines at the lower level.

There are plenty of information boards describing how the stone crushers and cutters worked, as well as the geological history. Although the quarry is now disused, in its day it produced huge amounts of paving and building materials. Indeed, it was said that Macclesfield was not paved with gold, but almost entirely with stone from Tegg's Nose quarry.

To leave the hill, continue south along the track for 400m, passing the old quarry and a track that leads off right, to a point where a path leaves backwards to the left. It goes downhill to a seat; then turns SE and zigzags its way down the hillside, emerging on to the track at the bottom, where you go left through the gate, re-joining the short route. Now return to the narrative on page 33 at *.

Walk 5 – Three Shires and Three Rivers

NE along Clough Lane, following Clough Brook, past Clough House to pick up a track following Cumberland Brook, and up to Danebower Hollow. Having crossed the main road, return is along the River Dane, Three Shire Heads and over the moor to the lane down from the A54.

Distance and climb	9 km (5.8 miles) and 340m (1100 ft), taking about three hours
Grading	Grading: Moderate, climbing gradient 1 in 9, children friendly
OS map	Landranger 118
Start	Off-road parking area by Wildboarclough bridge From the A54 Congleton to Buxton road, take the lane going northwest, signposted to Wildboarclough, 2 km (1.5 miles) northeast from Allgreave. Keep left on the way down the hill, and then parking is under the lee of the rock face opposite the bridge

The walk

Before you start, look at the plaque on the bridge, commemorating the flash flood of 1989. Like several others in historical times, it was caused by a violent thunderstorm over the catchment area of the various streams that contribute to the flow along Clough Brook. The weather accounts suggest that the area received about 10 cm (4 inches) of rain in two hours (close to being a UK record), and the catchment area is about 24 sq km (10 sq miles). After a bit of maths and some experiments to measure the speed of a stream in flood, I worked out that, about two hours after the storm, the water at the bridge (where the valley is

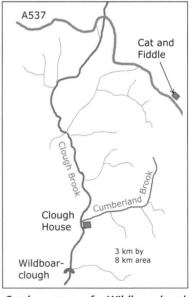

Catchment area for Wildboarclough

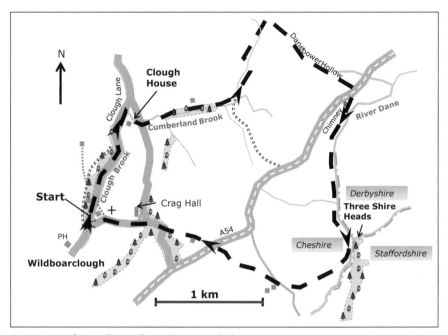

Route Map for Walk 5 – Three Shires and Three Rivers

at its narrowest) would have been over 5m (15ft) deep - well above the parapets. Sure enough, the old pictures of the disaster show the water-mark high up the rock face at the parking spot. The bridge was badly damaged, the lane was washed away, properties were inundated, and it was six months before the repairs were completed.

To start, follow the lane for 1.5 km (a mile) going north, with Clough Brook always by your side, crossing and re-crossing under the road. It's usually quiet, in the lee of Shutlingsloe to the NW, and with pleasant pastures on the east side. There's a parking area at the Clough House farm. Walk through that and up the short hill, crossing Clough Brook where it's joined by the second river on this walk, Cumberland Brook. Then cross the lane and go though the gate ('Public Footpath to Cat and Fiddle'), with Cumberland Brook on your left.

As you walk up hill there's a footbridge and then a wooded area, and it's nice to look back occasionally at the unfolding views to Shutlingsloe. After the wooded area you reach Cumberland Waterfall and a gate, with a fingerpost beyond. Two tributaries join around this area, coming off Wood Moss and Dane Bower, and it's apparent how the water accumulates from all directions as it drains from the moors, each stream cutting its own vee-shaped gully as the thousands of years pass by.

From the fingerpost, follow the direction to the Cat and Fiddle, walking by, or sometimes in, the Cumberland Clough stream. The ground is rocky sandstone, with black coal outcropping along the path, and you soon have to ford the stream and tackle a steep scramble on the other side. Best is to use the short rocky gully that

I passed these alpacas – I just love the fringe and the piece of straw

goes left, then turn back right as the path becomes evident again, reaching a wall gap at the top. Then it's plain sailing on a grass moor path, crossing Cumberland Clough yet again and looping back to reach the track along Dane Bower Hollow, where you go right.

Up to that point, the moors are draining SW down Cumberland Clough, but once past the high point on Dane Bower Hollow, the water oozing from the peat hags on the other side is destined for the Dane, to the SE. It's to that third river that you're heading, visible in the valley as you cross the main road and shin over the crash barrier. Its source is up the valley to the left at that point, beyond the Danebower quarries, at Dane Head, alongside the lane that crosses Axe Edge Moor. I worked out that, in normal weather, water leaving Axe Edge arrives in the Irish Sea, via the Weaver and the Mersey, about three days later.

From the road, it's a scramble down the slope, across a track and past the chimney to a walker's gate, where you will follow the grass path going downhill to the riverside. The chimney was the furnace vent for the boiler that powered a haulage engine, dragging coal from the old Dane Bower Mine, now capped and abandoned (in 1922) below your feet. Later, by the river, you'll pass by more stone remnants of mining buildings and walls.

Three Shire Heads

The path by the Dane is well managed, with paving. It used to be extremely wet, even during long dry spells. It leads to one of the most photographed beauty spots in the Peaks – Thee Shire Heads, where the counties of Derbyshire, Cheshire and Staffordshire meet at the splendid packhorse bridge. In the 19th century, when policing was a county responsibility, it was a convenient place for the bad guys to step over the boundary and evade pursuit. Perhaps they even stood on the other side and catcalled at the helpless constabulary – I don't know.

From Three Shire Heads take the path on the right of the river, going SW and uphill, around Cut-thorn Hill. It leads to a gate, where you cross the lane by a property and take the stile opposite, ready to follow the grass moor path around Birchenough Hill. At one point, the path swings left and crosses a stile, where I think you get the best view of Shutlingsloe. Evidently, others do as well, because someone posted a photo on Google Earth® that was identical to mine. We must have been only minutes apart on the day. (It was late winter 2010.)

The best view of Shutlingsloe?

From the stile, the path (sometimes wet) winds down to the main road and continues on the other side, where it crosses more wet areas on platoon bridges. With good views to the fore, you reach a gate leading to a short downhill track through Leech Wood and on to the lane, where you go right and follow it back to the car.

Walk 6 – Errwood Reservoir

South alongside the Goyt, uphill, crossing a packhorse bridge and coming back north on the other side, before following a path up to Goyt Lane. Return is via Bunsal Cob, the dam and alongside the reservoir. At the dam there is the option to walk up 'The Street' lane (steep) and return via a shrine and the Errwood Hall ruin.

Distance and climb	7 km (4.4 miles) and 280m (900 ft), taking about three hours, or 9 km (5.8 miles) and 420m (1360ft) for the optional longer route
Grading	Easy to moderate, climbing gradient 1 in 11, children friendly. Moderate for the longer route, with a climbing gradient of 1 in 9
OS map	Landranger 118
Start	Goyt Valley – Errwood Hall car park The Goyt Valley is 5 km (three miles) west of Buxton. The easiest approach is off the A5004 Buxton/Whaley Bridge road, down the lane from Long Hill, or from Kettleshulme on the B5470 Macclesfield/Whaley Bridge road. The lane coming from the A537 Buxton/Macclesfield road, passing Lamaload Reservoir, is narrow and steep, and you cannot approach from Derbyshire Bridge because the lane alongside the River Goyt is one way only

The walk

Walk south from the car park, alongside the top of the reservoir, and then the Goyt, soon a long way below you. Think about the reservoir. When they flooded the valley in the 1960s, what did they drown? The answer is in the sketch, but I think

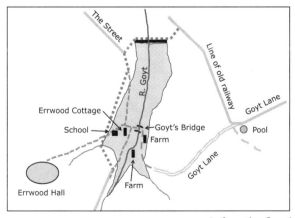

Before the flood

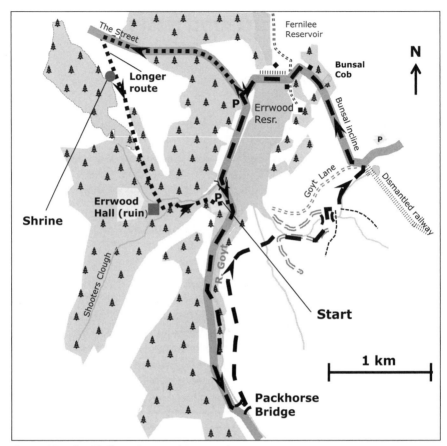

Route Map for Walk 6 – Errwood Reservoir

most of the buildings were demolished before they let the water in.

In the sketch of the flooded village, the solid lines are existing lanes, including the Goyt Lane track, and the dotted lines are new lanes that came with the reservoir construction. The dashed lines are lanes as they were, making a crossroads, with a school, cottages and farms nearby, and a track to the hall. From The Street to Goyt Lane was a salt trail, and the packhorse bridge (Goyt's Bridge) dates back over 300 years. (I think the hamlet was also called Goyt's Bridge.)

Goyt's Bridge was marked by the Ordnance Survey in about 1880, with a height of 262m (851 ft) above sea level. The reservoir surface, when full, is at 288m (936 ft), which makes it at least 26m (85 ft) deep. Thoughtfully, they preserved the bridge, rebuilding it up stream on the Goyt, and you will cross it as part of this walk.

About 1 km (half a mile) from the start you reach a fingerpost and gate on the left, where you can take the path down to the river, marked 'Waterside Walk'. It's very pleasant, with a few benches, and it emerges again on to the lane after 600m, near the old Goytsclough Quarry. Allegedly, the haulage company Pickfords started trading from there in the 17th century, but with packhorses, not removal vans. Quarry stone went out, and other goods came back, so the beasts were always burdened with full panniers.

Packhorse bridge

You'll soon spot the packhorse bridge in the valley below, crossing the river. Walk down to it and have a look around – there's a small plaque. Since the original bridge had an Ordnance Survey mark on one of the stones, it struck me that I should be able to find it. I couldn't, despite examining every nook and cranny. It would have been a small bronze rivet hammered into one of the ridge stones on the parapet. The stones certainly look 300 years old, so I'll concede that they did use the originals and not simply pinch some from the nearby quarry. Maybe they re-laid the ridge stone with the rivet upside down.

Over the bridge, go left along the path. You quickly reach a crossing path with a fingerpost – go left towards Wildmoorstone. The path follows the river, going north, with some muddy areas and some walking boards, and it may be overgrown in summer. It runs close to a wall, first on the left side, then crossing over as it turns NE, and it's from that area that you get the best views of the reservoir.

The path reaches a broad track at a bend – go left there, walking 500m to the iron bridge over Wildmoorstone Brook. On the other side, go right on the path, from the bend. There's a potentially muddy area with some boards, then the path forks. Keep left there, alongside the boggy tributary, walking uphill to the corner of Goyt Lane. There, the disused Cromford and High Peak Railway joins from the right and goes on down the hill to the reservoirs as the lane.

The pool at the top was created by the railway embankment acting as a dam, providing water for the stationary steam engine that pulled the wagons of the steep 1 in 7 Bunsal incline. It was one of nine such inclines on the route; too steep for the running engines. The section was abandoned in 1892. (The route of the old railway also features in Walks 7 and 8.)

From the top, go left, down the hard lane (not the Goyt Lane track). Initially, this Bunsal incline was negotiated in two steps, with a second stationary engine half way up. The water supply pool for that is in the trees on the right as you walk down, now overgrown. At the bottom (Bunsal Cob) there is a roadside plaque explaining more of the local history.

After that, the lane turns west, crossing the dam. When I was there in early July 2010, the water was very low, well below the spillway, so that the sailing club had difficulty launching their yachts, and the citizens of Manchester and Stockport were enduring a hosepipe ban.

On the other side of the dam (where there is a plaque giving some facts and figures) you turn south, following the road by the water back to the car park, crossing Shooter's Clough Bridge on the way. But you do have an

Errwood Reservoir – depleted

option instead of turning right from the dam and walking up The Street. It's 1.5 km (one mile) steeply uphill until you reach a gate and stile on the left, signposted to Errwood Hall and Foxlow Edge. That path soon divides – keep right, on the lower route, and look out for the curious shrine (300m on from the road) below you on the right.

It was built by the Grimshawes, the owners of Errwood Hall, and dedicated to a certain Miss Dolores, a member of Spanish nobility who returned to England with the family after one of their many jaunts abroad. Whether she was governess, friend or mistress is unknown, but whoever she was, she

Miss Delores' shrine

merited a very personal memorial. Look inside, it's always open to the walking public and it's still used for Parish communications. But beware; it can be very claust-rophobic.

After that brief spiritual experience, continue on the path, going SE along the edge of the wood. Keep right at the next fingerpost, and you eventually reach a bridge over Shooter's Clough. Cross that and go left on the other side, up the steps and around to the site of the ruined hall. The Grimshawes built it in the mid-1800s, no doubt with money earned from the sweat of a thousand labourers, trading in cotton, coal and paper. It was demolished in 1930, in anticipation of the coming reservoir (to reduce the risk of pollution).

From the ruin, continue south for 50m on the path you arrived on; then double back left, downhill on a track. That leads back through the rhododendrons to the car park.

Walk 7 – Fernilee Reservoir and Windgather Rocks

Across the Errwood dam and north along the east side of the Fernilee Reservoir, before crossing the Fernilee dam and continuing north on the west side of the Goyt. Return is via Taxal Edge, Windgather Rocks and The Street lane. A shortcut is available from the Fernilee dam through the plantation on the west side of the reservoir.

Distance and climb	9.5 km (5.9 miles) and 340m (1100 ft), taking about three hours, or 5 km (3.1 miles) and 130m (420 ft) for a shorter route
Grading	Moderate, climbing gradient 1 in 10. Children need supervision at Windgather Rocks. Shorter route is easy, climbing gradient 1 in 16
OS map	Landranger 118
Start	Goyt Valley – Car park near Errwood dam The directions are the same as those given for Walk 6, except that parking is in the small car park near the west end of the Errwood dam

The walk

From the car park, walk across the Errwood dam to the east side. On the way, peer through the gap in the hedge on the north side, roughly in the middle. As far as I can see, that view is the best outlook you'll get of the reservoir from above.

On the east side there is the Errwood bell-mouth spillway and the valve-house. Then, when you walk down to the track that runs alongside Fernilee, you can take the walker's gate and have a closer look at the bottom of the dam. The spillway emerges from a tunnel (dry when I was there in July 2010) and a continuous outflow wells up from the underground culvert, controlled from the valve-house. Unlike some of the very complex reservoir layouts you will encounter in later walks, Errwood and Fernilee are very simple.

Walking on north, the path alongside the reservoir follows the route of the old Cromford and High Peak Railway, continuing towards Whaley Bridge (Walk 8) from the bottom of the Bunsal incline (Walk 6). The railway pre-dated the Fernilee reservoir, which was built in 1938, thirty years before Errwood. The old OS maps, from before the valley was flooded, show Fernilee Mill in the valley bottom, a gunpowder factory that killed its employees on a regular basis.

The track reaches a gate, leading on to a metalled road. At that point, an old track joins from the right, coming down across the fields from the A5004, and the 1922 OS map shows that continuing down to the mill, with a tramway and a bridge over the Goyt. To prevent any possibilities of pollution, all that would have been demolished before they flooded the valley.

Fernilee dam has a broad spillway for wet conditions, and the valve-house allows some water to the ongoing River Goyt and controls the outflow to the water purification works in the valley below. That water

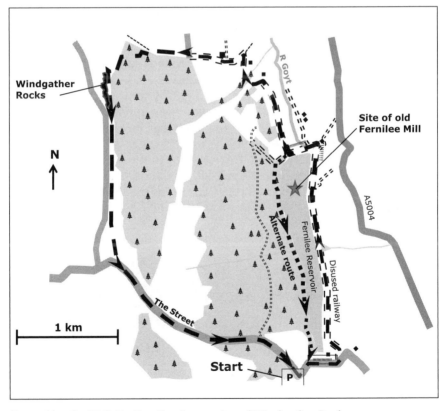

Route Map for Walk 7 – Fernilee Reservoir and Windgather Rocks

then goes on to serve the people of Stockport and some surrounding areas, but not Manchester. That gets its water from reservoirs to the north. When you look at the size of Fernilee and Errwood, both with 30m (100 ft) high dams, the volume of water is enormous. But even that supplies only one modest centre of population.

I worked it out. (Please excuse the Imperial units.) The two reservoirs hold 2000 million gallons between them and the catchment area in the hills around them delivers (on average) 3000 million gallons per year (8 million gallons per day). So the rain can fill them both from scratch in eight months. What matters is the amount coming in – the 3000 million gallons – because that sets the limit on what can be taken out, no matter how big the reservoir is. But if the reservoirs were too small, they'd fill up too quickly and waste much of the water down the spillways; so size is important.

From the information on the Errwood dam plaque, it seems that 330,000 people (probably more by now) need 17 million gallons per day (50 gallons each per day), so another 9 million gallons must come from other reservoirs. When you multiply all this nationwide, you can see just how much water we need, and a few weeks of drought can be a real problem.

To continue the walk, cross the dam to the west side, where there is one option to go left alongside the trees and enter the wood at the walker's gate, where the main track turns right and goes uphill. This is the short route back, where you follow the forest path and look for the 'Waterside Walk' leaving to the left. It leads to the water's edge, so there are at least some views other than trees, and follows close to the reservoir all the way back to the Errwood dam, where you walk up the right-hand corner to the lane above. (On the way, don't take any side paths that leave right from the waterside path.)

Fernilee Reservoir from the NE end of the dam

The longer route that takes in Windgather Rocks goes right from the west end of the Fernilee dam, on the limestone track following the west side of the Goyt (low down in the valley), and with a wooded area on the hillside to the left. After 800m the track bends left and descends, curving round at the bottom, over a stream, and rising up the other side to Madscar Farm. There, take the track that rises steeply to the west side of the farm (you may have to open the gate) and turn back sharp left by the fingerpost at the top, walking on 200m to pass Overton Hall Farm on the right.

Windgather Rocks

From the farm, continue west along the road, beginning the ascent to Taxal Edge. After 400m the road comes to a cattle grid and a track. Go straight across, following the path up and across the moor, with the forest on your left. At a fork in the track, keep left, and then left again to cross a ladder stile at the edge of the trees. The path then follows the wall for 200m before veering left at a fingerpost and cutting through the forest, crossing a stream on a small footbridge. At the other side, as you leave the trees, go left over the stile and follow the wall until it veers right and takes the path up to Windgather Rocks.

As you walk on south along the top of the rocks, there may well be some rock climbers; it's a very popular spot for the beginners, before they progress on to the harder climbs. Obviously, it's a spot to keep a wary eye on the kids. The name is very apt. I visited on a calm day, but on the edge the wind was blowing hard, coming unimpeded from the west.

The path keeps to the top, with the lane visible to the west, and eventually reaches a gate and then follows the wall on the inside all the way to Pym Chair, marked by a line of posts. It's much better than walking along the lane. About 400m before the Pym Chair car-parking area there's a stile from the lane, with a path going diagonally to the left, with more posts. Follow that; it cuts the corner to The Street lane, which takes you back down to the car.

Walk 8 – The Peak Forest Canal and Eccles Pike

The route follows the canal to the end of the Buxworth Basin, then the ancient tramway to Whitehough. Return is via the viewpoint on Eccles Pike and on to New Horwich, passing the Roosdyche historical feature.

Distance and climb	**8.2 km (5.1 miles) and 250m (800 ft), taking about 2.5 hours**
Grading	**Easy to moderate, climbing gradient 1 in 7, children need supervision by the canal**
OS map	**Landranger 110**
Start	**Whaley Bridge – Canal Wharf car park** **Whaley Bridge is off the A6 Stockport/Buxton Road, on the B5470 from Macclesfield and the A5004 from Buxton. From the A5004 in the town, take Bridge Street opposite the Jodrell Arms pub, then turn immediately left along Canal Street, running beside the main road. It goes right and right again to a free car park**

The walk

Whaley Bridge is a junction of road, rail and canal. One hundred years ago it was a hive of activity, transferring goods and materials between the three modes of transport, in particular limestone and coal.

The start of the walk is at the old Transhipment Warehouse (1832) at the beginning of the canal – the 'Whaley Bridge Basin', north from the car park. It's a listed building, and there are plenty of information boards there, and elsewhere along the canal, that relate the local history.

Look at the front of the building, car park side, through the railings. You can see the water bubbling up. It comes from a feeder, having run 3 km (two miles) from the header reservoir at Combs, dropping 60m

Transhipment Warehouse

Route for the Combs canal feeder

(200 ft) on the way (1 in 60). Somewhere, it is joined by another feeder from Todbrook Reservoir, west of the town (height 188m – 610 ft), but I couldn't figure out how, since the final section is in a culvert.

I visited the Combs dam. Even though the reservoir was half empty, the feeder was flowing swiftly, a channel about 1m wide and 0.5m deep. Then it follows the B5470 as on the map. And, somehow, it crosses the Goyt – I think it must go under it, rather like a 'U-bend'. The Victorian engineers were certainly ingenious!

At Whaley Bridge, the canal is 157m (510 ft) above sea level, and as it winds NW there are no locks until it reaches Marple, where it drops another 60m (200 ft). So the bubbling water you see by the warehouse is trying to keep up with the water lost when boats use those locks. In late July 2010, even though some welcome rain had arrived, it looked like the reservoirs were struggling to keep up the supply. Indeed, the Leeds/Liverpool canal had to be closed for that reason.

For the walk, follow the towpath north, with the River Goyt below, in the trees. Excess water in the canal is drained over weirs, either into the Goyt or into Black Brook, which is close by on the Buxworth leg. You turn down that leg by crossing the footbridge where the canal divides, then walking east (right) on the well-made path.

Cross the Goyt, then pass under the A6, the traffic noise giving you a scare as the vehicles rattle the expansion joints on the road above. Next is a loop, with an overspill into Black Brook, followed by the Canal Side Cottages and the newly renovated Wharfinger's House (the man in charge of the wharf). Finally, there is the Buxworth Basin, superbly restored, with scope for wandering around and looking at the information boards. I particularly liked the three-dimensional display, pointing out the positions of the old limekilns, the tramway and the cantilever crane. Limestone came down from the quarries, using horse-drawn wagons on the tramway, and that was processed by the kilns into quicklime, which had many uses.

Looking across to the south side, by the lane that bridges the canal, the large stone structure is part of an old kiln, vandalised when they built the

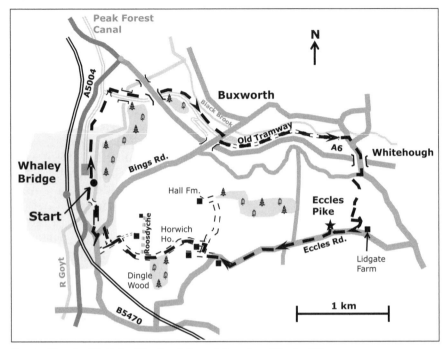

Route Map for Walk 8 – The Peak Forest Canal and Eccles Pike

A6. A local Senior Citizen told me she remembered the lane passing under a tunnel formed by the kilns.

From the Basin, keep on the north side, walking east past the Navigation Inn and picking up the Peak Forest Tramway. It's never too far from the noisy A6, passing through a wooded area and a gate with an officious notice (which does not apply to walkers). Next is an uninspiring industrial site, only partially softened by a water feature as you emerge on to Lower Lane.

Part of a limekiln

Go right there, following the lane SE to join Whitehough Head Lane at a pub and telephone box, where you keep straight on and cross the

A6. 300m on from the A6, go right down Back Eccles Lane ('Single Track Road' – and note that the 50K OS map might be inaccurate for that location), following it 150m to a right-hand bend, with a track continuing straight on ('Byway open to all traffic'). Follow that track uphill, eventually passing through a gate and joining a crossing bridleway, where you go left (signposted to Lidgate and Crossings) to reach Eccles Road. Go right there, with 600m of quiet lane walking to reach the stile to the viewpoint on Eccles Pike.

It's a fabulous spot, with a 360 degree panorama. There's a ground mounted topograph (which might well be stolen), so you can pick out the landmarks for yourself, but I'll highlight Combs Reservoir to the south, with the flat-topped Combs Edge behind it. Although you can see the reservoir dam, the canal feeder outlet is hidden by trees.

Having enjoyed the view, continue west along the lane. It's 1.5 km (a mile) downhill, with a pleasant outlook to the south, until you reach the newly converted cottages at Horwich Farm, where the lane turns sharp left. Carry straight on from that corner, on the track, then right after 50m, by Horwich Lodge. Round the back, take the stile and then follow the right-hand side of the wall. The path leads round the Horwich House farm, through a gate and along a track by a disused and forlorn cricket pitch. The view left is to the mast on Ladder Hill, and the view to the fore is to Whaley Moor, behind the town.

There are a couple of gates as the track skirts Dingle Wood, before you reach the 'Roosdyche' feature, the tree-lined avenue to the right, behind the iron gate with a 'Private' notice. The boring explanation for the feature is that it was cut by Ice-Age melt-water. More interesting is that it was a human Bronze-Age settlement, or even a Roman chariot-racing stadium. I like that last one the best.

Walking on down the hill, there is a view of the Todbrook Reservoir dam, and to the left is a new cricket pitch, presumably replacing the old one. The track turns left, to become a lane (New Horwich Road). After 50m, by the first building, take the public footpath to the right, between the walls, emerging on to Bings Road, where you go left down to Old Road. Go right there, and immediately right again through the gate on to a grassy track.

This is part of the route of the old Cromford and High Peak Railway, dating to 1831. (You also use sections of it in Walks 6 and 7.) Whaley Bridge was the rail terminus, linking the Cromford Canal near Matlock with the Peak Forest Canal. What they couldn't manage with another canal, because there was not enough water, they achieved with a railway.

But it had nine steep inclines (one is discussed in Walk 6 – Errwood Reservoir), and the track soon turns left and goes down one of those slopes. There are a couple of stone features mounted in the ground that must have been part of the railway. Here, they used horses to pull the wagons up the incline, tethered to a shaft and a set of gears at the top (a Horse Gin), and with chains running down the hill.

At the bottom, ignore the road bridge on the left and carry on a few metres to the splendid old iron bridge where the railway crossed the Goyt on its way to its final destination at the Wharf. (The object sticking up by the left parapet is a railway signal counter-weight.) Then the car park is on the other side.

Iron Railway Bridge over the Goyt

Walk 9 – River Dove and High Wheeldon

This is more about the view of a river valley than the walk by the river itself. That view is spectacular - in fact, I think the panorama from the top of High Wheeldon is one of the best in the Peak District.

The route follows the River Dove from the village, to the ancient Pilsbury Castle. Return is then on the high ground (open access), including High Wheeldon, that overlooks the valley from the NE.

Distance and climb	6.5 km (four miles) and 250m (820 ft), taking about two hours
Grading	Moderate, climbing gradient 1 in 6 (two stiff climbs), children need supervision on High Wheeldon
OS map	Landranger 119
Start	Lane side, Crowdicote Crowdicote is 1.5 km (one mile) east of Longnor, 10 km (six miles) south of Buxton. Longnor is on the B5053, which runs from the A515 at Brierlow Bar to the A523 Leek/Ashbourne road. Parking is roadside, on the narrow lane that leaves north from the village, about 50m from the junction

The walk

Take the metalled lane that leaves SE from the village, indicated to Bridge End Farm. It's not a right of way at first (an official path joins it from the fields off the lane to Longnor), but the residents told me that everyone goes that way. As you pass the farm, the right of way proper begins and the route then follows the River Dove, first on the track and then across pastures to Pilsbury Castle.

The river is only 8 km (five miles) old at that point, with the source to the NW off Axe Edge, coming under the A53 trunk road near Leap Edge. So it's nothing special to look at or walk along. In Walks 12 and 13 you will see it in a more dramatic phase.

Also, Walks 10 and 11 visit the River Manifold, just before it joins the Dove at Ilam. For this current walk, at Longnor, the two rivers are very close, the Manifold having started at Flash Head just south of the source

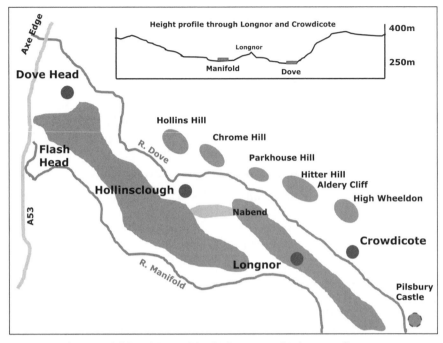

River map for Manifold and Dove (Shaded areas are high ground)

of the Dove. The sketch shows the river routes, and the profile of the terrain between them at their closest point. If you could make a tunnel some 20m below Longnor, about 800m long, you could get the Manifold to pour into the Dove. That would annoy the Manifold tourist attractions downstream when it completely dried up!

Pilsbury Castle is impossible to miss, with the limestone outcrop forming one side, and the information board providing some useful background. It probably held a garrison, and would have commanded the valley route. The limestone outcrop is interesting – a handy back wall defence. It's actually a small coral reef, formed under the sea millions of years ago

Pilsbury Castle

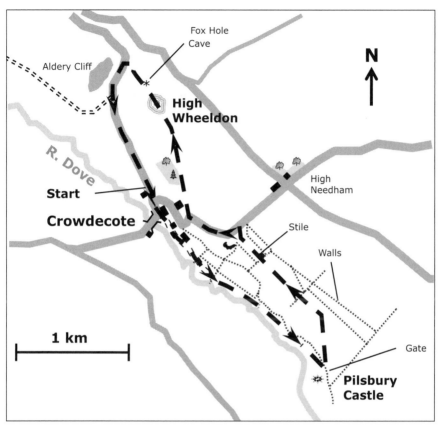

Route Map for Walk 9 – River Dove and High Wheeldon

and subsequently uplifted. You will see larger versions later in the walk. Then the other side is bordered by the river, an important source of water for the castle.

To leave the site, take the walker's gate in the wall to the NE, marked with a white arrow and to open-access land. On the other side, walk diagonally up the slope, keeping on a due north direction. To help, behind you in a field is a rusty barn, due south. So walk away from that.

It's a stiff climb, and after about 400m you'll reach the higher ground flanking Waggon Low, with a crossing wall and fence. That is the limit of open-access land, where you turn left (NW) to walk along it. It turns briefly SW, before going NW again (as shown on the map), where there is a fallen wall to stride over (no fence). 600m on is a reassuring stile, with another white arrow, to bridge a crossing wall, with then just one field (250m) before the lane. The final part of that is marked with, I think, remnants of mining, and there is a dewpond by the wall (bone dry in 2010). Keep right there to find the last wall stile to the lane.

Go left on the road, round the right-hand bend and downhill to the sharp left-hand bend. From the corner, take the gate back into open-access land and head straight for High Wheeldon, which you can see to the fore, with a pillar on top. It's 900m away. There's a shallow valley to cross, a wall stile, and a steep bit at the end, before you can stand on the top.

High Wheeldon is a splendid viewpoint, and an obvious place for the

Descending High Wheeldon

Ordnance Survey pillar. Looking NW (as in the picture) there is the Dove valley going up to its source, with the sequence of limestone reefs to the right. In the foreground is Hitter Hill, with Aldery Cliff just in view, and next in line is Parkhouse Hill and Chrome Hill, both with sharp ridges.

On the other side of the valley, the nose of high ground is Nabend, with Hollinsclough Moor beyond, keeping the River Manifold in its own valley. As you scan the Dove valley below, going south, it appears 'U'-shaped, as if formed by a glacier. But there is no glacial basin at the head (Axe Edge), so the valley was widened by the river, not ice.

To leave, continue down the spine of the hill, the path becoming very steep. Once Aldery Cliff is in view, about 40m on from that point look for 'Fox Hole Cave' to the right, just below the path. It's gated, and looks nondescript. But it has produced some remarkable archaeological finds; worked antlers (tools) from 11,000 years ago (near the end of the last Ice-Age) and human remains (a burial) from 6000 years ago.

Near the bottom you might have to slide down on your backside – better that than slipping. With Aldery Cliff to the fore, keep right when you reach a wall, tacking diagonally down to the final path to the stile on to the lane. Go left there and follow it 1 km (0.6 mile) back to the car.

Walk 10 – River Manifold – Wettonmill and Ecton

North on a track by the east side of the river, to The Lee and Ecton. Return is on the west side, via the Swainsley tunnel. If you shortcut from The Lee to the tunnel, the route is reduced to 4.3 km (2.7 miles).

Perhaps you could do this walk and Walk 11, which has the same starting point, either side of lunch on the same day. That's why I've kept it short and simple.

Distance and climb	**6.4 km (four miles) and 180m (600 ft), taking about two hours**
Grading	**Easy, climbing gradient 1 in 13, children friendly**
OS map	**Landranger 119**
Start	**Manifold Valley – Wettonmill (as for Walk 11)** **The best approach is off the B5053 that runs between the A515 Buxton/Ashbourne and the A52 Leek/Ashbourne roads. Take the lane signposted to Butterton and Manifold Valley; then follow the signs to Ecton. Out of Butterton, go right down the single-track road signposted to Wettonmill and Manifold Valley. It's narrow and steep. When you reach the junction at the bottom, parking is to the left**

The walk

Go briefly south from the parking spot and cross the bridge, with Wettonmill on the right. It's a National Trust site, but just a café at present, with some useful information boards. The mill last ground corn in the mid 19th century, and is in the process of restoration. Maybe you could take your lunch there between the two walks; or even picnic as you watch the ducks on the river.

Wettonmill – always busy

The Manifold (meaning 'many folds') rises near Flash and joins the Dove at Ilam. Down to Wettonmill it is a full stream, but like many limestone rivers it has a habit of disappearing, which you will see later in Walk 11. But when you lean over the bridge you should see plenty of water, whatever the time of year.

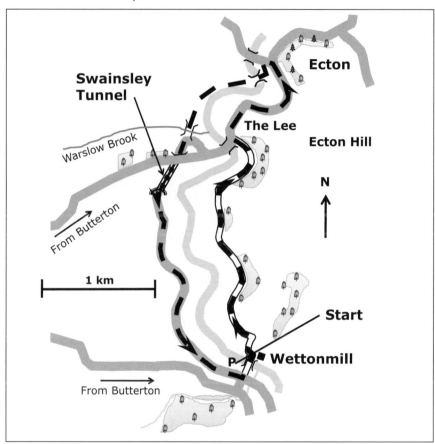

Route Map for Walk 10 – Manifold Valley – Wettonmill and Ecton

From the café side of the bridge, go left up the track; then turn left in front of the farm, signposted to Hulme End. 100 years ago, this track would have been the main thoroughfare along the river, superseded now by the path on the west side. Its importance is confirmed by a sequence of Ordnance Survey marks on some of the gateposts, made in about 1880.

(They are engraved arrows with a line above). It leads to the lane at The Lee, the river always close by.

There, the river is flowing over dense Ecton and Hopedale Limestone, having traversed impervious shales further north. Just south of Wettonmill, the bedrock changes to more porous Milldale Limestone, and you will see the effect of that later in Walk 11.

At The Lee, if you've a mind to take a shortcut, go left on the lane (signposted to Wettonmill and Butterton), over the bridge, then right (to Wettonmill), ready to turn back through the Swainsley tunnel. Otherwise, go right (signposted to Ecton), with Ecton Hill overshadowing you on the right. It's famous for its old copper mines, yielding very rich ores, enough to make the Fifth Duke of Devonshire most of his money. He did spread it about a bit, though, particularly in Buxton, where there is now the Royal Devonshire Hospital.

Swainsley Tunnel

It's 1 km (half a mile) to the village – a modest collection of dwellings, where you turn left down the lane indicated to Warslow, and immediately left again down the gated path. This is the reclaimed narrow gauge Leek and Manifold railway, running from Hulme End to Waterhouses, a quaint local facility that transported milk, corn, chickens and tourists along the Manifold Valley. It operated between 1904 and 1934, linking with the main railway system at its southern end. The favourite station for the tourists was Thor's Cave, and you get to visit that in Walk 11.

The path follows the course of the river, through the trees, emerging in front of the Swainsley tunnel after crossing Warslow Brook. Allegedly, the tunnel was constructed so that the high and mighty in the nearby Swainsley Hall wouldn't be inconvenienced by the smoke and the noise. It just shows you the influence of Edwardian gentry. It's quite well lit, but it's used by traffic, so you might have to take cover in one of the 'refuges' along the side. It's also darker than the picture suggests.

From there, it's a pleasant stroll along the road back to the parking spot. All you have to do is dodge the cyclists.

Walk 11 – River Manifold and Thor's Cave

South on a lane and track by the west side of the River Manifold, with an excursion to look at the river flow, then crossing to make a steep ascent to Thor's Cave. Return is via a concession path to Wetton, a descent on the lanes to Weags Bridge and a walk north along the track by the river.

Perhaps you could do this walk in the afternoon, having completed the easy Walk 10, which has the same start point, before lunch.

Distance and climb	7.5 km (4.7 miles) and 280m (900 ft), taking about three hours
Grading	Moderate, climbing gradient is 1 in 8 (one stiff climb), children need close supervision at the cave
OS map	Landranger 119
Start	Manifold Valley – Wetton Mill (as for Walk 10) The car route to the walk start is the same as that described for Walk 10

The walk

Go south from the parking spot, but unlike Walk 10, don't cross the bridge, keep straight on along the lane (the old Leek and Manifold Railway route, signposted to Wetton) as it runs fairly close to the river. After 200m there's a gate into the rough pasture on the left, bordering the river. It's private land, but you'll usually see a clear path where many visitors have made the brief excursion to the water's edge.

It's generally the area where the river disappears, so you can stand in the middle of the stream with the water coming towards you, only to see it fade away around your feet. If the weather has been wet, then some water may be flowing on, to disappear within the

Manifold disappearing

next 400m. There has to have been a real monsoon for the river to be flowing above ground along the rest of the valley.

So where does it go? Down fissures in the bedrock, called swallets, is the answer, sinking into the porous limestone and re-emerging downstream near Ilam, 60m (200 ft) lower. As shown in the sketch (where the vertical scale is exaggerated), from Wettonmill north, the bedrock is denser, so the water is held at the surface. South of Wettonmill, the water builds up in the porous bedrock, emerging again when

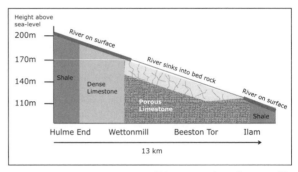

Dissappearing river profile

it is blocked by the impervious shale under Ilam. The River Hamps, which joins the Manifold by Beeston Tor, suffers the same fate, usually disappearing just after Waterhouses.

Walking on, the lane crosses the river on a flat railway bridge, with only a three ton capacity. So it really was a 'light' railway. Looking over that bridge when I visited in early July 2010, the bed was bone dry. However, the Google Earth® Street View car must have visited after a summer deluge, because the river was flowing then.

When you reach the Leek Road lane, go straight over the gated bridge, crossing the river again and continuing on the route of the old railway. Within 1km (half a mile), the mouth of Thor's Cave is gaping down from above – an impressive sight. It's limestone, with the cave cut by swirling water, dissolving the rock. But it

Thor's Cave

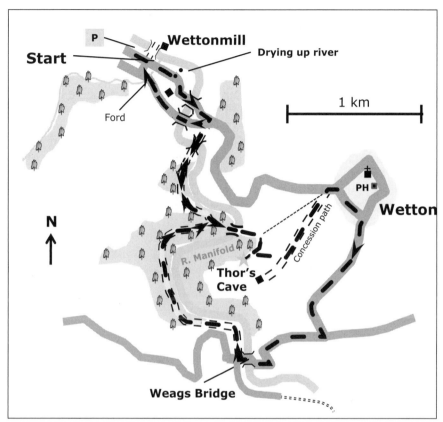

Route Map for Walk 11 – Manifold Valley and Thor's Cave

didn't happen up there. Eons ago, the area would have looked very different, with the Thor rocks part of a wider landscape, with many underground streams carving out the caves. Then the surrounding rocks were eroded away, leaving the Thor outcrop standing, with its cavern.

To get up there, cross the river on the footbridge, with a useful information board on the way, and follow the steep path up through the wood. Mercifully, there are steps. Then go right up more steps, indicated to Thor's Cave.

From the mouth, the view down the valley is splendid, and inside is equally impressive. The limestone is slippery, but it's worth the effort, and it's obvious why early man found it a secure refuge. Apparently, when the cave was first investigated, the mouth was widened to its present size from a much smaller opening. Inside, there is a second opening – the 'west window' – with a 100m drop if you poke your head out. Don't do it!

To leave the cave, look for a narrow, level path that runs east from the top of the upcoming steps. It goes round the outcrop (with a path also leaving it to the right, one that goes up above the cave), through a gate by a tree, across a shallow gully and up the other side to a wall stile on to a track. That takes you to Wetton, and is a concession path to and from the cave.

It joins Leek Road, so you could return to Wettonmill down that, going left (2 km – 1.3 miles). But my route goes right up Leek Road, then right again after a few metres, signposted to Grindon. Before I left the village I had a look around. It seems that Wetton's main claim to fame is the annual toe-wrestling contest at Ye Old Royal Oak!

Leaving that vision behind, continue on the lane to the tee-junction, where you turn right (Carr Lane). That eventually goes steeply downhill and joins Larkstone Lane, where you go right and downhill again, reaching Weags Bridge. This route down from Wetton is quiet, with good views,

View from Thor's Cave

and it's not worth taking any of the cross-field shortcut paths that are shown on the OS maps. Near the bottom of the hill, I met a large party of sixth-formers walking up. They were whining and moaning, asking how far it was to the top. They had about nine-tenths still to go, but I lied, saying they were nearly there and that there was a good pub. They'd be disappointed of course, or even frustrated and angry – but it's all good character building stuff!

From Weags Bridge (where the Manifold is likely to be bone dry), go right, back on the route of the old railway. You'll join the outgoing route under Thor's Cave, but when you cross the gated railway bridge again on to Leek Road, go left, up to the road bridge. That area is the Redhurst Swallet, where any water that escapes the Wettonmill Swallet usually disappears. After that, there is the bridge and, just before Wettonmill, a ford to wade, which was the one of the reasons for taking you that way!

Walk 12 – Ilam and Dove Dale

On a field path to the mouth of the dale, along Dove Dale as far as Ilam Rock, then crossing the river to leave the valley via Hall Dale. Return is along a lane, up to Ilam Tops and on to the Bunster Hill summit, dropping steeply down to the car. The shorter walk takes a very steep path from near Ilam Rock to the pastures on the west side of the valley, reaching Ilam Tops from the east.

Distance and climb	9.8 km (6.1 miles) and 280m (900 ft), taking three hours. A shortcut is available, reducing the walk to 7.1 km (4.5 miles)
Grading	Moderate, climbing gradient 1 in 10, children need close supervision at some points. The shortcut has a very steep 1 in 4 climb
OS map	Landranger 119
Start	Ilam – roadside, on the lane to Thorpe Ilam is best approached from the A523/A52 Leek/Ashbourne road. Take the Blore lane that leaves NE from the A523/A52 junction, NW of Ashbourne, following it 3 km (two miles) before turning left down a lane signposted to Ilam and Dove Dale. That winds down to the village, with splendid views of the walk area. At the memorial, go right up the Thorpe lane; then parking is roadside on the right after 150m, opposite the walker's gate to Bunster Hill

The walk

Take the gate on to Bunster Hill and follow the path east across the fields, parallel with the lane. It's well marked, with stiles, and you pass the Izaak Walton Hotel on the right before dropping down through some trees to a drive that leads to the Dove Dale car park. Go left there, along the road marked with no vehicle access, which is the way into the dale.

Stepping stones

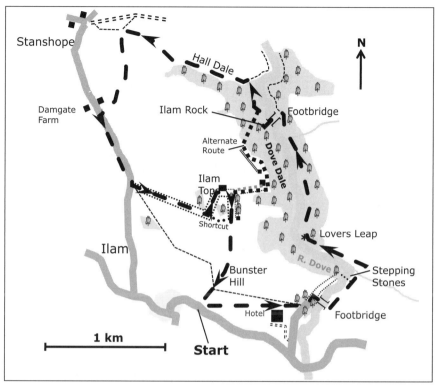

Route Map for Walk 12 – Ilam and Dove Dale

After the water-flow monitoring station there is a footbridge and some information boards. There, if you keep on the left side of the river, on the road, you will have to cross later by the stepping-stones. If you don't fancy that, use the bridge and follow the other side, picking your way over the shiny limestone and the screes cascading down from Thorpe Cloud.

The stepping-stones are a centrepiece, one of the most photographed locations in the Peak District. As many as 8,000 walkers have been logged past them in one day, and they mark the point where the dale turns north. You follow the river on its right, though glorious scenery, with striking rock formations and caves. It's all limestone, cut when the river was a deluge after the last Ice Age, leaving monuments of harder rock still standing as softer ones were washed down to the sea.

It's not long before you climb a set of polished steps, with an equally shiny outcrop at the top, overlooking the valley. It's Lover's Leap, but now it gets used as a seat and a photograph opportunity, so it's not just boots that polish the stone. It's a place to keep an eye on the kids, obviously. Apparently, the heartbroken young lady who leapt off the edge survived the fall, her skirts making a parachute and catching in the tree canopy below. That doesn't seem right to me – doesn't someone have to make the ultimate sacrifice for the outcrop to claim the official 'Lover's Leap' qualification?

With a nice orange source, perhaps?

Walking on, there are the Tissington Spires and the Natural Arch rock formations, a boarded section as the path is squeezed by the river, and you eventually arrive at the footbridge and the Ilam Rock spire. I captured a climber, nearly at the top. They must be mad.

Cross the bridge; then pop your head into the low cave on the opposite bank. Even if it's summer, the temperature inside is freezing. Go right from that (north – 'Public Footpath to Ilam'), walking 250m before you reach another fingerpost. The main walk goes on to Stanshope, but you have the

Climber on Ilam Rock

option there of the shorter walk by going left ('Ilam – Steep Ascent'). If you are taking that route, turn to the end of this narrative for directions.

Following the main route, you cross a wall stile to reach a fingerpost indicating left to Stanshope, along Hall Dale. It's stony at first, but soon becomes a grassy path, steadily levelling as you approach Stanshope. You can carry on to the track just before the hamlet if you want, then walk south on Ilam Moor Lane. I chose to take the diagonal field path that leaves the Hall Dale path just after a lone bush, 250m before Stanshope.

To do that, cross to a gate, follow the left side of a wall over stiles, keep straight on across the open field when that wall veers right towards the farm, go over another wall stile, and then along the left of the next wall, reaching a pair of trees. There, go diagonally across the field to the top right-hand corner, over a stile, along the left of the wall to the next stile, then diagonally across that field to the lane. (Anywhere on that route, you might be confronted by mud or cows.)

Walking along the lane, south of Damgate Farm you will pass one track going right, one drive going right (with a track opposite) and a track left (to Hill Top Farm). Then you want the next drive to the left, to Ilam Tops Farm, guarded by a cattle grid. Follow that drive, even though the official paths use the grass. After it has crossed another cattle grid it swings left to the farm, where you reach an avenue of trees going right (south). That is the right of way, but it looks like most walkers carry straight on after the cattle grid (The 'shortcut' indicated on the route map), through the next gate, then keep left alongside the walled plantation to reach the gate at the south end of the avenue of trees.

* From the south end of the tree avenue, keep to the left of the wall, continuing south (the direction of the avenue), even though the OS map shows a right of way going SW. The south path is clearly conceded, because it leads to a wall stile into the open-access area of Bunster Hill, with the National Trust sign. Now you make for the summit, and return to the car down the spine of the hill. It is a splendid end to the walk, with views all round the west and south, including the Manifold Valley and the Ilam Hall estate.

Like Thorpe Cloud, and several other hills in the Peak District (see Walk 9, for instance), Bunster Hill is an old limestone coral reef, heaved up from under a primeval sea many millions of years ago. It's rich in fossils – have a scrape around on your way down; see if you can find one. Then, if you have any time left, consider a look round Ilam Park and the hall – it's very pleasant.

Shorter route

From the fingerpost, take the very steep path up though the wood. It reaches more level ground, keeping just inside the trees, eventually emerging into pastureland via a stile. There, the official path keeps low, skirting along the upper area of the wood, but there is a field track higher to the right that I used. It leads to a farm gate, which is private; walkers then skirting round the left of the farm site and the main residence, rejoining the official path. Then take the marked footpath gate on the

Descending Bunster Hill

right to reach the main farm drive that comes from the Ilam Tops property. Just before that property, go left up the avenue of trees to the end – a clump of trees and a building, where you intercept the main route.

Now return to paragraph * on the previous page of this narrative.

Walk 13 – Biggin Dale and Wolfscote Dale on the Dove

East from the village on the Heathcote lane (Hall Lane), taking a track towards Biggin and then turning down Biggin Dale. Return is along the Dove via Wolfscote Dale and a section of Beresford Dale. A torch will be handy on this walk.

Distance and climb	10 km (6.2 miles) and 280m (900 ft), taking about 3 hours
Grading	Grading: Easy to moderate, climbing gradient 1 in 9, children friendly
OS map	Landranger 119
Start	Hartington village Hartington is NE from the A523 Leek/Ashbourne road, on the B5053 and then the B5054 after Warslow. Alternatively, go west on the B5054 from the A515 Buxton/Ashbourne road

The walk

Hartington is a beautiful village, catering for the walking tourist with pubs, cafes and shops. I parked by the pond – a splendid location, with ducks and geese waiting to be fed. Nearby is The Old Cheese Shop, with quality produce to tempt you.

To start the walk, go east from the centre, past the village store, and turn right up Hall Bank, by the telephone box and war memorial. There's a shop on the corner with excellent pork pies for extra provisions. Near the top of the hill you pass Hartington Hall, a Youth Hostel with excellent family facilities. Opposite, is a track (a 'leisure lane') to Dove Dale. Ignore that and continue along Hall Lane for another 200m to a second track leading off right, called Highfield Lane, and marked to 'Biggin, Cycle Route 54'.

As you follow that SE, take note of the stone walls. They are at least 400 years old. Consider any one stone. When was it last part of a hillside? Probably 500 years ago. How was it cut? By stone chisel and hammer, perhaps helped by a bit of saltpetre. How did they get it from the quarry to the site? Mule and cart, without doubt. Just imagine the labour to build even a short section of such a wall - we don't know we're born!

1 km (half a mile) along Highfield Lane there's a track going left, then another going right. Look over the wall on the left, opposite the second track, to see a small stone circle, with six flat stones. I could find no references about it, but it must surely mark an ancient burial or meeting place, probably more than 3000 years old.

Walking on from there, the track reaches a lane (Liffs Lane) by some properties, where you continue SE for 200m to the path leaving on the right to Biggin Dale. It's National Trust, and open-access land - pleasant walking along the wall. Even the sewage farm has a point of interest - the final sampling point at the end of the treatment line looks like a giant

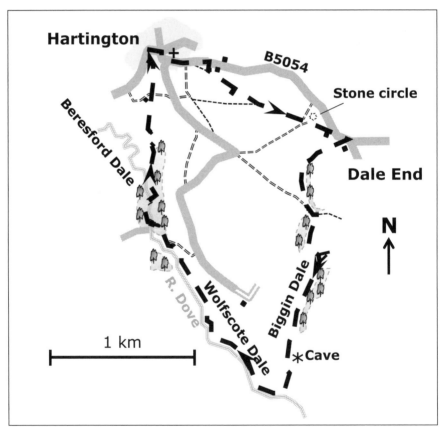

Route Map for Walk 13 – Biggin Dale and Wolfscote Dale

hypodermic syringe, with a wheel to turn, all designed to ensure that nothing but the cleanest water continues down the dale.

A 'Biggin' is a form of hat, worn in the Middle Ages, or some sort of building, so that the dale is named after the nearby village. There are several 'Biggins' in the UK, so I'd bet on the building definition. As you walk on down the grassy path, the dale is vee-shaped, so it was cut by water, not ice. Where is the stream now? I'd guess that it was a temporary torrent emerging from the retreating glaciers 10,000 years ago, slicing its way through the bedrock in just a few hundred years.

As you approach the bottom there are some old walls, either dwellings or stock enclosures. Like the stone circle, I could find no references, but I'd guess they could be more than 1000 years old. At the bottom, with a wall to your front, keep left and look for the walker's gate that takes your round the dewpond to the other side of the wall. The dewpond is nicely preserved – they were sealed with clay and used to collect rainwater (there is never enough dew) for sheep and cattle. They date to Saxon times.

My walking colleague, looking the part

After the pond, go right (SW) along the left side of the wall, the path leading to a wooded area. It's here that water begins to appear, seeping from the hillside and rising from below ground – typical of limestone country. After emerging from the trees you'll come to a stile on the left, with a small mine entrance. It's called an Adit; a horizontal shaft that either followed a vein of lead, gave easy access to a mine initially dug from above, or was simply an exploratory dig. Take a look inside. How far can you get in the dark before your nerve fails you? If you have your torch, you should be able to reach the end – but I'm not telling you how far! There are no hazards, other than water underfoot and a low, hard rock ceiling. Curiously, my colleague spotted a used prophylactic near the end – the mind boggles!

Walking on, the path broadens and passes a newly renovated dry-stone wall. People actually pay for the privilege of doing that work! Then it's not long before you reach the River Dove, where the route goes right along Wolfscote Dale. It's a splendid walk, with limestone spires and screes, and

Wolfscote Dale in early spring

with the gentle river. It's managed by a series of weirs, and stocked with brown trout for people who like that sort of thing. The meaning of 'Wolfscote' is not clear; 'cote' is usually a small dwelling, but it can also be a hill slope (from the French). Wolf could mean the animal (and there would have been some in the area hundreds of years ago), or a derivative of a person's name.

As you walk, look at the screes. They are similar to those in the Dove Dale walk (Walk 12) - inevitably, since the river and the rock are common to both walks. Do screes all over the country lie at the same angle? It always looks to be 45 degrees to me. Or does it depend on the size of the stones? (Just some more trivia for you to consider!)

After 1.5 km (a mile), the valley broadens, and there is another small cave in the cliffs on the right to poke your head into. It has a chimney at the back, going up into sinister blackness. Then there's a track leaving uphill to the right. Don't follow that; keep left by the river, over a narrow stream and through a wall stile into the meadow. At the other end of that meadow, cross the river on the footbridge and then turn right, following the left bank through Beresford Dale. This is more like a gorge, with a spire rock sitting mid-stream. It's called a 'Pike' (sitting in 'Pike Pool'), as named in the late 17th Century by Charles Cotton, the owner of the now ruined Beresford Hall, out of sight amongst the trees high on the left.

After the Pike, cross the water again and follow the other side, turning uphill and away from the river, eventually emerging into meadows. The path is easy to follow, with marker arrows, crossing a track through two wall stiles. It was lambing time when we did this walk, and all the lambs were numbered, together with their mothers. My colleague ventured a humorous theory that it was done so the ewes could find their lambs! My argument against it was that the ewe would not be able to read her own number on her back, so it wouldn't work!

From there, the path goes along the back of farm buildings and turns left through a walker's gate and out into the village, with the car soon in sight.

Walk 14 – Bradford Dale and Youlgreave

West along Bradford Dale, crossing the river and coming back east through woods to Youlgreave centre. Return is via lanes to the Lathkill river, into Alport, and back west on the Bradford.

Distance and climb	6.1 km (3.8 miles) and 140m (440 ft), taking about two hours
Grading	Easy, climbing gradient 1 in 13, children friendly
OS map	Landranger 119
Start	Roadside, Bradford Road out of Youlgreave, by the river Youlgreave can be approached from Parsley Hay on the A515 Buxton/Ashbourne road, using the lane that passes the Arbor Low henge and following the signs for Middleton and Youlgreave. From the east, off the A6 Buxton/Matlock road, take the B5066 from just south of Haddon Hall, then turn right for Alport and Youlgreave. In Youlgreave, go south on Bradford Road from the church, and park at the bottom. There's room for about a dozen cars on the lane side

The walk

The Bradford is one of the shortest rivers in the Peaks, about 8 km (five miles) from its source on Gratton Moor (south) to its confluence with the Lathkill in Alport.

Fancy a swim?

Go west through the gate ('Unsuitable for Motor Vehicles'), following the path on the right-hand side of the water. Unlike the Manifold and the Hamps, this limestone river keeps above ground, with nicely managed weirs and pools. They are the 'Bradford Dams', dating to the 1890s, made for fishing the brown trout. If you watch by a patch of still, clear water, you're bound to see one.

The first pool invites you to have a swim, but I wasn't tempted. Next is a gate and stile, with a footbridge beyond. Cross that and continue on the other side of the river as far as the old stone bridge, about 1.5 km (a mile) from the start. Cross that, follow the path briefly as it starts to climb, then take a path leaving right, going along the north side of the river, back eastwards.

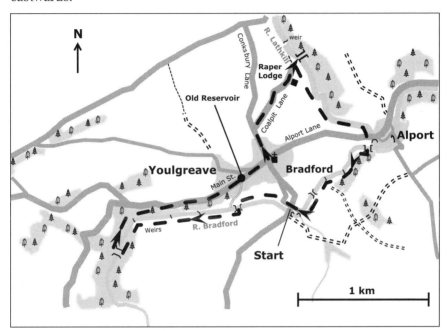

Route Map for Walk 14 – Bradford Dale and Youlgreave

There's a wall stile and a few steps as the path takes you near the water and then uphill through the trees to emerge on to Main Street, by the allotments. From there into the village is pleasant walking, usually quiet, with the main point of interest (from the perspective of this book at any rate) being the unusual village reservoir, now a fountain.

In 1829, each night it collected 1500 gallons (5000 litres) of water

Youlgreave village reservoir

from the nearby Mawstone spring so that the villagers could use it through the day. In those times the population was about 300, so that's five gallons each, less than one tenth of what we might personally use today. Still, they didn't need much; they only had to drink it and cook with it. Flushing water closets were in their infancy, and the daily bath had yet to be embraced by the wider populace.

At the church crossroads, go left, signposted to Over Haddon, and follow the lane for 300m to the right-turn down the narrow Coalpit Lane ('No Through Road'). It was here that I passed a field of cows, all lying down chewing the cud, totally at leisure. Every one was facing either NW or SE; no other direction. What's that about? The Earth's magnetic field? The sun? Herding instinct? (Sorry, I just can't help worrying about such things!)

Follow Coalpit Lane to the end, by Rapper Lodge, where you will go right through a walker's gate on to the field path along the valley. Before you do that, walk on and have a look at the bridge and weir at the River Lathkill – it's a good spot for a snack and a picture. (You can't follow the Lathkill on its east side, which is disappointing.)

Bridge and limestone bluff on the River Bradford

The field path takes you to Alport, via a few stiles and gates, emerging on to Alport Lane. Cross that, by the telephone box, and take the drive from the white gate. The Lathkill is to your left, with the Bradford joining it to your front. There's another white gate; then you cross the Bradford to follow its south side.

There's more pleasant walking, and on the way you pass a massive limestone cliff (called a 'bluff'). Look at it closely – it's 30m (90 ft) high, according to my rough estimate – see if you can spot any fossils. Limestone is a sedimentary rock, made from billions of tiny sea creatures that died and sank to the bottom of a warm, shallow ocean. Their calcium-based skeletons were covered by billions of their friends, building up in layers as the eons went by. Eventually, the weight from above crushed them into the hard rock you see now, subsequently uplifted from the sea by movements in the Earth's crust.

How long to make that 30m of rock? My guesstimate, thinking about the yearly thickness of dead creatures on the seabed and how much they have to be squashed (ten to one, I'd say, like snow into ice), is at least one million years – probably a lot more. And that's a mere blink in the Earth's history. It certainly puts our lifespan in perspective.

Walking on, there is a kissing gate, with a track joining from the left, and another picturesque spot with a bridge and a seat under a bluff. Don't cross that bridge; carry on along the river, eventually crossing it again before you reach the gate on to the lane where you're parked.

Walk 15 – Lathkill Dale

South on a lane down to Lathkill Dale. Then 3km (two miles) alongside the river to its cave source, before a steep climb up to the top and a return via Haddon Grove and the lanes.

Distance and climb	**9.5 km (5.9 miles) and 310m (1000 ft), taking about three hours, or 7.4 km (4.6 miles) and 200m (700 ft), taking 2.5 hours, for the children's route**
Grading	**Moderate, climbing gradient 1 in 6, and 1 in 7 for the children's route**
OS map	**Landranger 119**
Start	**Over Haddon, east of Monyash** **From the A515 Buxton/Leek road, follow the B5055 east through Monyash and on for 4 km (2.5 miles), taking the lane signposted right to Over Haddon and Lathkill Dale. There is a pay and display car park in the village (off Main St), and other parking might be difficult. The full walk is not suitable for young children, but the indicated shorter route is OK. There is an opportunity to climb down a ladder at one point, where parental discretion is required**

The walk

From Main Street, walk down the 'No through road' lane to the valley. At the bottom, don't cross the stream by the weir, carry on along the limestone track on the right of the water. But that weir is important - take note of it. As you walk on, there's an information board, one of many providing interesting facts about the area.

It's pleasant walking by the water, and after 250m you'll see a channel merging with the river

The Old Engine House

alongside the path. It's called a sough (pronounced 'suff'), and it accompanies you for 400m before turning underground up the embankment. Here, look for a path up though the trees to a ruined building, with steps, some interesting information boards and the old Mandale Mine to peer into.

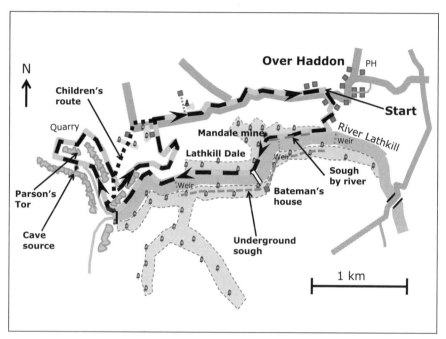

Route for Walk 15 – Lathkill Dale

It's all about lead mining, and it's fascinating to see how the early miners (called 'Quaker Adventurers') got rid of the unwanted water. They dug the sough and pumped the mine water into that, initially using the wheel as a pump. They powered that with water brought along a leat, tapping off the river further west. So they were using water to lift water, taking 50 years over the project. The water wheel was later replaced by a beam engine pump, but that worked only briefly before the mining became uneconomical.

Returning to the path, after 100m you pass the remains of the aqueduct that carried the leat, with just the pillars standing. Then 250m further on there's a footbridge to a ruined building; Bateman's House. Step inside – there are more useful information boards to read.

This is another pump-house, drawing water from even deeper mines, and round the back there's a shaft with a ladder. At the bottom there're more information boards and a handle to turn, lighting up the deep shaft behind the safety railings. Listen for water running at the bottom. That's another sough, completely underground, and another huge labour for the miners. It drains the deeper mines, running from west

Remains of Bateman's House

of where you're standing to emerge at river level near the weir I mentioned earlier, forced up by an impenetrable barrier of basalt.

So why doesn't the Lathkill river water end up in the sough? A lot of it does, seeping through the limestone bed, so much so that, in times of drought, this section of the river will run dry. In April 2010 the river was running, but later in the year, after the long dry spell, there was no water anywhere except in the lower sough, which I could hear running.

Having crossed back over the bridge, continue following the river. You'll pass a splendid weir, go through a walker's gate and over a wall stile, now in an area where the path is more narrow and stony. (I think the area near the walker's gate is the western limit of the underground drainage sough.)

As the dale bends right, there's a bridge going left ('Sheepwash Bridge'), leading to Cales Dale, where a significant amount of the river water originates. To the right at that point is a set of steps climbing the steep slope, and later, when you come back along the top, the route reaches the top of those steps. If you have young children, climb those steps now and pick up the route at paragraph * on page 86.

If you're continuing on at the bottom, the dale opens out, with the impressive limestone crags, and at the right time of the year you might spot some wild orchids or the rare 'Jacob's Ladder' flowers.

400m on from the bridge and steps, a spur valley leaves right, tapering up to the high ground above. Above you, at the junction, Parson's Tor overlooks the valleys, and later, as you walk along the top, you'll appreciate just how the drunken Rev Robert Lomas died in 1776, when he was on his way home from the ale house.

It's also a spot to reflect on the geology. The dales are vee-shaped, so they were carved by rivers, not ice. So where is all the water that cut such

Limestone makes some great outcrops

a dramatic gorge? If it's been wet, there might be a trickle in the river, but that paltry flow couldn't have done the job. I can only conclude that the valleys were cut by a deluge coming off the melting glaciers at the end of the last Ice Age. Crossing the hard gritstone to the north, they would have made only a modest impression, but once the water got a foothold into the softer limestone, a gully could be cut very quickly. Imagine a river raging down Lathkill Dale, joined by another coming down the spur, heaving over the top, making a waterfall and producing a churning whirlpool where you're stranding. It probably took less than a thousand years to create the valley.

Now there's only a trickle, and if you walk on another 100m and

Lathkill source – dry as a bone

look to the left, there is the cave source of the river ('Lathkill Head Cave'). It was dry when I visited (late April 2010), despite all the snow we'd had, which seems to be the norm. Of course, the real source of the Lathkill is the higher pastures above the cave (around Knotlow, between Monyash and Flagg), with the rainwater percolating through the limestone and finding its way to the cave outlet.

Carry on beyond the cave for another 500m, to a wall stile. On the other side take the steps going up to the top. It's hard work, but brief, and well worth it to get a new perspective on the dale. Near the top you reach a footpath sign. Go right there, over the wall stile. Then you can follow the path along the edge, with splendid views into the dale.

The path runs alongside a wall and turns left up the spur you saw from below. At the corner is the grass ledge where the vicar rode his horse off the edge. Don't go near it! Instead, continue round the spur and on along the top. To your right is always a drop, either steep grass or sheer rock faces. It's not a children friendly section.

* 500m from the spur, you'll come to a walker's gate on the left, with the Sheepwash Bridge visible far below and the steps coming up from the valley (the children's route). You could take that gate, cross the pasture and paddocks the NE, and go through Haddon Grove Farm on to the lane, where you would go right, with 2.5 km (1.5 miles) to the car. Although the public footpath was not impeded, I found the combination of horses, dogs and campers rather intimidating. However, this is the preferred route with young children.

Nicer is to carry on along the top of the dale (turning right from the top of the steps, if you've just come up them). The path continues by the wall, via a stile and a walker's gate, before you reach a section of wooden fence (marked 'Private Land – No Access') and a lone tree, where the fence turns left. The path turns with it, but veers diagonally down the slope, into another spur valley. In the bottom there is a track. Head for that, then follow it uphill again as it winds back from north to south, then turns west through some trees and finally goes through a gate on to a track that takes you through Mill Farm. Once on the lane (which is quiet, pleasant walking), you go right, picking up the route from the shorter walk and with 2 km (1.3 miles) back to Over Haddon.

Walk 16 – Chee Dale and Miller's Dale on the River Wye

On a track and lane to Wormhill, a descent across pastures into the Wye Valley, and return via the disused railway and riverside. The anti-clockwise route allows an excellent view of the valley before dropping into it. The stepping-stones and the waterside terrain in the gorge are not suitable for young children, and it's these elements, rather than the gradient, that make it a moderate walk. Do not attempt it when the river is in flood, since the stepping-stones may be overtopped. However, since the Chee Tor tunnel is now open, you have an option to use that, avoiding the difficult river stretch.

Distance and climb	7.7 km (4.8 miles) and 280m (990 ft), taking about two and a half hours
Grading	Moderate, climbing gradient 1 in 11. The section along the river is difficult, where children need close supervision
OS map	Landranger 119
Start	Miller's Dale Station car park Take the B6049 north from the A6 Buxton/Bakewell road. Turn sharp left up the lane signposted to Wormhill, just before the railway bridge, with the pay and display car park then on the left after the two bridges. From the north, the B6049 leaves the A623 Chapel-en-le-Frith/Baslow road at Lane Head, reaching Miller's Dale via Tideswell

The walk

From the car park entrance off the lane, take the steps in the NW corner, signposted as a public footpath. They lead to a narrow walled path, going westwards past the stationmaster's house, rejoining the lane via a wooded area. The path is a very old route, and I'd guess it lead to Knot Low on the north side of the lane – an ancient burial ground.

Go left up the lane, walking 1.5 km (a mile) to the 'Wormhill – Please Drive Carefully' sign. On the way, with a clear view to the south by a field with a lone dead tree stump, look across to the meadows on the other side of the Wye Valley. You can just make out the lines of an ancient field system, raised ridges that, maybe in Roman times, would have been topped by palisades. (It helps if the sun is casting them in an oblique shadow, and they are very clear on Google Earth®.)

The walk route goes left over the stile just after the Wormhill sign, through Hassop Farm. However, before you go that way it's worth a look around Wormhill itself, a village with a history going back to 1066. It's a 500m stroll into the centre, where I got one of my best photographs. The village name could mean 'Wyrma's Hyll' (Old English) – a hill frequented by reptiles.

To find the village stocks, when you reach the lane that goes right to the church, follow the pavement alongside the meadow on the right. I researched into what could be thrown at miscreants in the stocks – believe me it was anything goes! Even horse dung and such like. There was none available when I was there, otherwise I would have practised on my walking colleague. (Nearby, there is also some interesting information about James Brindley, a talented water engineer.)

If I could have locked him in, I would have done!

Having got your own photograph, return to the lane corner and follow the route through Hassop Farm. There's one big gate in the yard, then the path continues via a wall stile opposite the barns, going diagonally across the meadow to another wall stile, then diagonally again to the corner of the next field. There, the stile has an obstacle on the other side that presents a serious hazard to male walkers!

From that mantrap, the path continues on the same bearing, across meadows to another stile and gate, before descending into Flag Dale, going right and down through the trees. It rises steeply on the other side to yet another stile; then you follow the line of the ruined wall on your left, crossing it and going round the end of the next ruined wall. From there, head for the gate in the far corner of the field, on to a lane.

The lane is the Pennine Bridleway, and you follow it south (left) and then SW through Mosley Farm (where there was a very sinister Frisian bull glaring through the wooden shutters of a barn – I understand they are

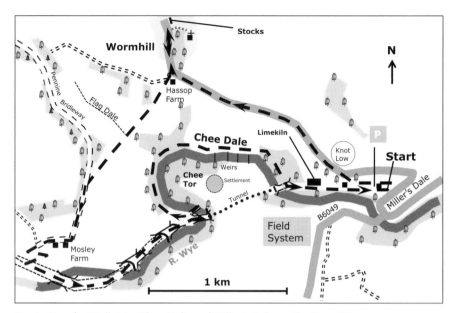

Route Map for Walk 16 – Chee Dale and Miller's Dale on the River Wye

the most dangerous). On the other side, as the farm track turns away north, take the grassy track going downhill to the south ('Bridlepath to Chee Dale'), with the Wye Valley before you. It's a splendid view, with the massive limestone buttresses, and the railway in the bottom.

The track makes a steep zigzag decent, emerging on to the disused railway track (gate to 'Alternative route to avoid river crossing'), where you go left – the ongoing route to the Monsal Trail, another part of which features in Walk 17. You actually join on a spur coming from Great Rocks Dale, and you soon merge with the main track that was once a busy line between London and Manchester. At the sides, the limestone rock is stained red with iron oxide – the so-called 'iron stone'. The river is well below you, with bridge

Stepping-stones – unusually dry

parapets to peer over, and there are two short tunnels before you reach the recently opened Chee Tor Tunnel. (On the summit of Chee Tor, by the way, is an ancient settlement – see the 25,000 Series OS map – no doubt connected to the field system to the SE.)

Don't go through Chee Tunnel. Take the wall stile on the right and follow the path down to the riverside; then turn back right (fingerpost to 'Miller's Dale') so you pass under the railway bridge above. Next is a footbridge to cross the river, followed by the stepping-stones along the rock outcrop. August 2010 they were dryer than I've ever seen them. (Note that, if the river is in flood, or you have young children, you can avoid the river section by continuing through Chee Tunnel. It's quite long and surprisingly cold, even on a hot summer day.)

The River Wye rises on the NE side of Axe Edge, and has major tributaries coming from Combs Moss. Then it flows through Buxton before negotiating the limestone gorges. To cut such a gorge as Chee Dale (at least 70m deep), like the limestone rivers further south, it must once have been an Ice Age deluge.

The section after the stepping-stones is dramatic, but difficult, with massive rock outcrops and tricky limestone walking alongside the water.

Miller's Dale Limekilns

Some sections can be muddy, and there is one short climb, with the river beckoning, that needs great care. The path goes round a stream inlet, across a small bridge – note how the stream ('Wormhill Springs') appears from nowhere, welling up out of the limestone rocks. There's another little footbridge, more water joining the main river, then you pass a nature conservation area and a footbridge to Blackwell (which you don't cross), before the path reaches the railway again, the high bridge towering over the river. It's a popular abseiling venue.

Walk up to the top, where the track comes from the other end of the Chee Tor Tunnel, and go left, passing the old limekilns. There's an information board, and it's well worth a look inside, allowing time for your eyes to acclimatise. Then, walking on, take the path that goes back on the left after 120m, up to the top of the kilns.

The two holes are now covered, but the circular railway track and the hopper are still there. Take a moment to imagine the 12-hour working days as the labourers tipped the coal and limestone into the furnace. Then, underneath, another team ladled out the caustic quicklime, loading it into the waiting trucks. It puts today's working life into perspective. (Looking south over the fence, you can again see the ancient field system on the meadow across the valley.)

From there back to Miller's Dale Station and the car is then a short walk. There're some picnic tables, and it's worth a look at all the information boards before you make for home.

Walk 17 – Monsal Trail and Litton Mill, on the River Wye

Along the disused railway, crossing the river at Cressbrook Mill and following the path by the water to Litton Mill. Return is over the high ground south of the valley, back to the railway, to make the walk a 'lasso' shape. That high path can be intimidating, with steep grassy slopes falling away into the valley. It's not a place for very young children, and an alternative return route is indicated. Also, like Walk 16, wet weather is best avoided, because the river can flood the path around the Cressbrook weir.

Distance and climb	8 km (5.0 miles) and 400m (1300 ft), taking about two and a half hours
Grading	Moderate, climbing gradient 1 in 6 (one stiff climb), children need supervision on the high section
OS map	Landranger 119
Start	**Monsal Head** Take the B6465 NW from Ashford in the Water (16 km – ten miles – east of Buxton on the A6). The Monsal Head Hotel, with a pay and display car park adjacent, is 2 km (one and half miles). I avoided the charge by parking on the lane into Little Longstone, a luxury that might not be available at peak season

The walk

The walk begins from the north side of the Monsal Head Hotel, through the wall stile and down the steps going right, finger-posted to the viaduct (the 'Headstone Viaduct'). Before you descend, take a moment to admire the view down the valley. You can see the viaduct, the disused railway (which will be the start and return route), as well as the river winding its way down from Buxton.

The path zigzags to the bottom, with the track emerging from the Headstone Tunnel to cross the viaduct, where there are some information boards about the old Midland Railway (That section of the walk also features in Walk 18, reversed). The last train was in 1968, but the route leaves us with some excellent walking.

View NW from Monsal Head

Following the track (The Monsal Trail), with views of the River Wye unfolding to the right, you soon reach the small Monsal Dale Station, with more information boards to read. Typically (nanny state), the notice entices you with talk of nearby lead mines, but then discourages you from looking into them.

It's 800m to the Cressbrook Tunnel entrance, where you take the stile on the right to the concession path along the side of the hill, with Cressbrook Mill (converted to apartments) in view on the other side of the river. After 100m a path forks left up the slope. Don't take it – it will be your return route later. (If you use one of the alternative return routes later, you will emerge from that Cressbrook Tunnel.)

Continuing on, the path drops down to the weir and bridge at Cressbrook, with the large millpond. It's called Water-cum-Jolly Dale – a beautiful spot. (I think the name might mean 'Valley with pleasing water' – but that's a guess.) You should keep left over the next, smaller, bridge (concession path) and then follow the river on the north side, below the impressive limestone buttress. I've been turned back at this point on

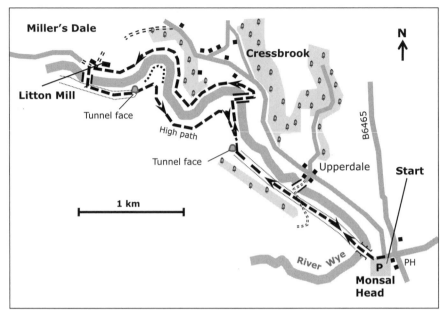

Route Map for Walk 17 – Monsal Dale and Litton Mill

previous walks, with water above my boots, but in spring 2010 it was as dry as a bone. If you're unlucky, you can escape to Cressbrook (look for the concession path notice) and then follow the lanes on the north side up to Litton Mill. (I provide some directions for this at the end of the narrative).

The path follows the river to Litton Mill, with one or two relics of the mill era on the way. The mill has a notorious history, abusing its workforce, using child labour, and generally fuelling my own prejudices regarding the Victorian textile industry. Now it's all residential apartments – best thing that ever happed to it.

About 400m before Litton, a stream joins the river from the right and accompanies you to the mill, steadily getting lower than the river. That's the millstream, and to explain how it worked, the water system is shown in the sketch.

It's confused by the fact that the main flow has been altered from the days when the mill was in full production, but I think I've got it right. The weir creates a large header pool, and most of the water was taken through the mill as the millstream, dropping about 7m (20 ft) inside the mill as it drove

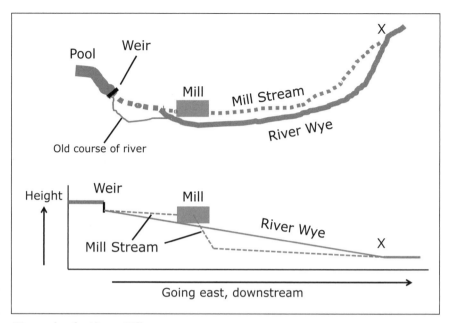

Water plan for Litton Mill

the wheel. The ongoing millstream then fell gently, alongside and below the main river. Meanwhile, the Wye, coming round the side of the mill, dropped steadily to the point ('X') where it and the millstream were at the same height again, about 400m on from the mill. Nowadays, only a token flow is allowed through the mill, with the main flow taken back into the river from just before the mill, rather than along the old course off the weir.

At the mill, look for the telephone box. 30m on from that, take the path left, alongside a property, signposted to 'Monsal Trail - Miller's Dale', crossing the footbridge and ascending the other side, back on to the old railway track. Go left there, following it to the Litton Tunnel, where there's an information board about the mill. (Here you have the option of returning through the tunnels, avoiding the high path - see the paragraph at the end of this narrative.)

For the main path, use the path that leaves to the side of the entrance. It's a steep climb, and it reaches a crossing path where you go left, the route then winding along the hillside, with a long, steep grassy slope into the valley. It's tricky when wet, and you wouldn't stop until you hit the river - so children need close supervision.

There are excellent views into the valley as you walk, including back to the mill, and at one point there is a break in the tunnels, the track emerging below before entering the Monsal section. Just before that is a rocky area – it's a spoil heap of material dug out when they made a vertical tunnel vent. Looking across to the north side you'll spot Cressbrook Hall, and then Cressbrook Mill comes into view again, this time from a

Cressbrook Mill from the high path

higher perspective, so you can see some of the mill workings.

Finally, the path descends to join the outgoing route, where you retrace your steps along the railway, over the viaduct, then left up the zigzag path to the hotel.

Cressbrook to Litton, should the river path be flooded

When you reach the lane in Cressbrook, go left, steeply uphill. A lane joins from the right, with the entrance to Cressbrook Hall on the left. Keep straight on up the hill. You join a lane coming in from the right, where you keep straight on again, with a sharp bend to the right before you pass a chapel. 150m on, take the track to the left, indicated to Litton Mill. It becomes a field path, going downhill to a wall, where you go left on a track, first south and then swinging back NW as you circumnavigate a hill. The track doubles back south yet again and becomes a lane as it reaches Litton Mill by the phone box.

Return from Litton to the start, to avoid the high path

To avoid the high path, use the Litton Tunnel to return. It is always cold, but there is a brief break before you enter the Cressbrook Tunnel and then back into the light for the final section home. Although the tunnels are a novelty, one is much the same as another, so the high route back is infinitely preferable.

Walk 18 – Monsal Dale and Ashford

The route follows the River Wye near the main road; then runs along Monsal Dale to the Headstone Viaduct and up to Monsal Head. Return is across the high pastures near the Fin Cop Settlement to Ashford. The short section from the viaduct to Monsal Head is common to Walk 17.

Distance and climb	9.9 km (6.1 miles) and 390m (1300 ft), taking about three hours
Grading	Moderate, climbing gradient 1 in 6 (one stiff climb), children friendly
OS map	Landranger 119
Start	Lay-by, A6 trunk road, 1.5 km (one mile) west of Ashford Ashford is on the A6 Buxton/Bakewell road, 16 km (ten miles) east of Buxton

The walk

Walk 100m east and cross the road; then follow the gated track ('Conservation Area') that leads to a bridge over the river. The buildings there are the remains of a mill ('Ashford Old Water Mill', I think), previously used for bone crushing, turning the remnants collected by the rag and bone men into land fertiliser. Most of the bones came from leather tanning, Sheffield knife handle trimmings and discarded bone buttons from textile factories.

The mill is supposed to be in the process of renovation, but I saw little evidence of progress. I was curious about the cable spanning the river on the east side of the bridge, from the small building to the support frame. Was it for hoisting bags of crushed bone across the water, to a waiting horse and cart? Or is it a more recent device? Also, the water depth marker post is very tall, implying that massive floods are possible, swamping the bridge and the weir.

Go immediately right from the bridge, in front of the mill buildings, where you can examine the old iron wheels. The path goes between the river and the old millstream (on the left – now a dry bed), to reach the weir. It's only about one metre high, with the millstream now blocked off,

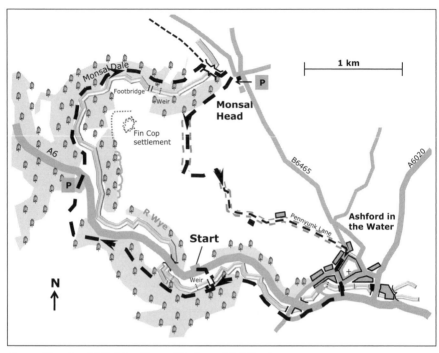

Route Map for Walk 18 – Monsal Dale and Ashford

so that the power to the wheels would have been modest; just enough to crush a few bones.

Cross the blocked off millstream and join the main track, going right. After 300m there is a stream appearing from underground, with a protective grill and a level measuring post. It's a sough, similar to those described in Walk 15. It comes from the Magpie Mine, which is 1.5 km (one mile) to the south, running underground below Sheldon. It was constructed in the 1870s, draining the lead mine and allowing more profitable working. In the 1960s it became blocked, building a huge head of water before the whole embankment burst out, above the present outlet. I wonder if anyone saw it – like the tree falling in the forest?

The path follows the perimeter of the wood, with views across the river to the Fin Cop hill on the other side of the main road. At the fingerpost that shows left to Sheldon, keep straight on towards White Lodge, going uphill through the wood to eventually reach a walker's gate and enter open ground. 200m on from there, at the marker post describing the

Common Rock-rose plant, go right, down the slope, and follow the track that is indicated (on a second post) to White Lodge Car Park.

After 200m there is an information board about Deep Dale, and a wall stile to the fore. Take that, going right on the other side; the path leading through a kissing gate, by Marianne Grace Wood and on to the car park. There's an information board to read; then you can make the difficult crossing on the main road to enter Monsal Dale on the other side.

Through the dale, follow the sign for Monsal Head, taking the grassy paths that keep close to the water whenever you can, for the best sights and sounds from the river. The weir makes a good photo, but it can be very dangerous when the river floods, overwhelming the rock shelf where I stood for my low angle view.

There is a sluice on the west side of the dam, presumably to relieve the pressure when the water is very high. But there is no sign of any old millstream taken from the top of the weir, and I could find no conclusive references to its historical use. People didn't dam up a river just for fun – it had to be for producing power or creating a fishing pool. Maybe that's the reason here.

Monsal Dale weir

Walking on, the viaduct soon comes into view. About 50m before it, take the path that leaves diagonally from the left, up to the old railway route; then go right to cross the viaduct, with the Headstone tunnel entrance to the fore. This stretch of the route is common to a section in Walk 17, and you take the steep path that zigzags left and right up to Monsal Head, near the public house.

At the top, don't go out on to the lane, keep on the path, signposted to Ashford and Monsal Dale. After about 20m, the path divides – keep left, to Ashford. It's wooded at first, with tantalising views into the dale, but it soon opens up, with the Fin Cop hill to the fore. There's a walker's gate (which you will go through), and a field gate on the right. It looks like some walkers use that to visit Fin Cop, which is an ancient Iron Age settlement (1000 BCE to 100 CE). It's a long earthwork dugout – best appreciated from the air than from ground level – with a recent dig revealing the bones of a pregnant woman, dumped and buried without due ceremony, probably around 30 BCE.

Continuing through the walker's gate, the track is called Pennyunk Lane, the ancient route that led up to the settlement. The name probably comes from Iron Age times, a pre-English or Celtic name approximating to 'Lands-end'. With the views to the east unfolding, the track leads south to a gate, with a dewpond nearby. 30m on from that, go left down a broad grass path along the edge of a field. Here, the left wall of Pennyunk Lane has been demolished, but the ancient track is intact again at the bottom, veering right after a gate. It's then 1.5 km (a mile) into Ashford, turning right and following Vicarage Lane down the hill from the end of the track.

Ashford is a picturesque little village, centred on the river, with numerous weirs and landscaped areas. Vicarage Lane ends at a roundabout; keep straight on there, down Fennel Street, to reach the old pump (with its arbour) and the 'Sheepwash Bridge' on to the main road. The pen where the lambs were placed is on the south side; then the ewes had to swim the river to reach them. It was an effective way of washing the fleeces before the ewes were sheared.

Cross the main road to the pavement and go right, walking 250m to the lane that goes left, indicated to Sheldon. Follow that for 200m; then take the public footpath to the right, by the river, with a weir close by. That path leads back to the old mill and the bridge, with pleasant water scenery to admire. It's much better than walking along the main road.

River scenery

Walk 19 – River Derwent and Froggatt Edge

Along the River Derwent to see Calver Weir, and onward to Grindleford Bridge. Return is on the high ground above the valley, along the Froggatt and Curbar Edges.

Distance and climb	10.4 km (6.5 miles) and 290m (950 ft), taking about three hours
Grading	Moderate, climbing gradient 1 in 6 (one stiff climb), children need supervision along Froggatt Edge and Curbar Edge
OS map	Landranger 119
Start	Curbar, in front of Curbar Primary School Curbar is off the A623 Chapel-en-le-Frith/Baslow road. 150m SE of the bridge over the River Derwent, take the road to the NE, signed to the Bridge Inn; then go right to park in front of the school

The walk

Walk by the pub and turn right up Dukes Drive (signposted to Froggatt and Sheffield), following it for 500m alongside the Derwent. As the river veers away, take the walker's gate on the left (fingerpost in memory of Mona Hartshorn), with the path keeping by the waterside all the way to Calver Weir.

It's a Grade II listed structure, going back to 1770, and recently renovated. It creates a header lake, with a millstream (called the 'Goit') tapped off the south-western side to operate the cotton mill at Calver. The sketch shows how it worked, with the height of the weir being about 3m, and with the river dropping by a further 4m by the time it gets to the mill. Running parallel from the top of the weir, the Goit falls only 3m to the mill

Calver Weir

entrance, then the final 4m inside the mill as it powered two wheels on its way back to the river. (I reconnoitred the walk on the other side of the river, by the Goit – it was nothing special, and the weir was out of sight.)

So it's a little different from Litton Mill in Walk 18, where the main mill stream was on the exit side of the wheel, but the result is the same. The wheel turned a shaft, and then numerous other shafts were driven from that by belts, operating the various spinning and weaving machines.

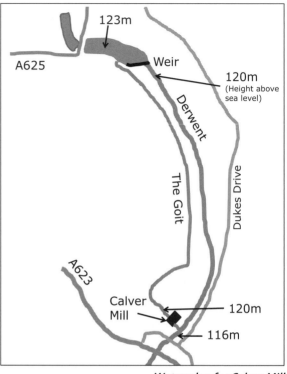

Water plan for Calver Mill

The two Calver mill wheels produced 160 HP, which is 120 kW, enough to power about 360 houses today. In Victorian times it kept 200 mill workers occupied, but 120 kW wouldn't come anywhere close to running the equivalent 21st century textile mill – where just one worker taps at a computer and the rest is down to technology and a vast amount of electrical power.

Why don't we use the mill today? Even though the electricity would be theoretically free, the initial costs are high, so it takes too long to get the outlay repaid – rather like home solar panels and wind turbines. Now the mill is converted to apartments; its final chapter I imagine. In the past it's been used as a film set for the TV *Colditz* series, so the residents might have to get used to some unusual 'tunnelling' noises. (The mill building is visible later in the walk, from the high ground.)

Walking on from the weir, the path reaches the main road by New Bridge. Go straight across the road there and continue on the right-hand side of the Derwent, on a well-made path. The river is wide and slow, held back by the weir, an influence that stretches back to beyond Grindleford.

As well as the river there are some pleasant landscaped areas on the right, before a wall stile leads on to Froggatt Lane, where you go left and walk on to Froggatt Bridge. Don't cross it; carry straight on along the Hollowgate lane, and then Spooner Lane from the corner as the main lane swings right. It becomes a track, an ancient byway, and part of the Derwent Valley Heritage Way.

It's pleasant walking, with good views left across the river to the high ground of Stoke Wood and forward to the Millstone and Burbage Edges above Hathersage. The walled track ends with a stile; then goes diagonally

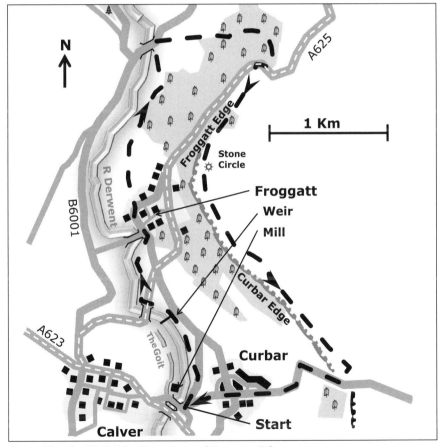

Route Map for Walk 19 – Derwent and Froggatt Edge

right when it's tempting to carry straight on, and you soon enter the National Trust area of Froggatt Wood. It's well maintained, with numerous streams flowing down from Froggatt Edge to feed the Derwent.

The path emerges on the other side, follows and then bridges a stream, before crossing a meadow to the lane coming from Grindleford Bridge. Go right along the lane for 30m; then turn right again up the public footpath track. After 300m, as the track turns right towards a property, keep left up the hill and into the trees, signposted to the Grouse Inn and Froggatt Edge.

After 200m, going steeply uphill, there is a crossing path with a metal cover at the junction. Below that is the conduit that takes water from the Laydybower and Derwent reservoirs (to the north) all the way to Derby and Leicester (south); a feature that is discussed more fully in Walk 21

Carry straight on upwards from that cover. After 150m, the path divides. Keep right there, and keep right again when you join a path coming from the left. Then another path joins from the left; keep right again, and you will soon reach the top. There's a stream to cross; then a set of steps takes you to the main road. Cross that, going right to a gate on the other side, ready to follow the path along Froggatt Edge.

Classic gritstone

At first, the path is shrouded by trees, and it's 800m (half a mile) before you reach a gate, where the view expands, with White Edge to the left and the Derwent valley to the right. 200m on from the gate, look out for the stone circle, about 30m off the path on the left. It was buried in ferns when I visited, so a good picture was impossible. In fact, it's a nondescript example – there are much better stone circles on Big Moor, the other side of White Edge. What were they for, made at least three thousand years ago? Opinion is divided, but I'd say they were meeting places, perhaps for ceremonies or worship.

From there to the lane beyond Curbar Edge is fabulous walking. I was lucky with a stunning day in mid September 2010, with a soft breeze, cotton wool clouds and clear air. The Gritstone rocks make fascinating shapes, the sedimentary layers, laid down all those millions of years ago, picked out by the wind and rain erosion. There may be climbers to watch (keep the kids away from the edge!) and you have a good view into the Derwent river valley. It's 'U'-shaped, steadily widened as the river has meandered over thousands of years, and you can see its onward route, south through the hills towards Baslow.

As Froggatt Edge gives way to Curbar Edge, keep to the high path along the top, ignoring any routes that drop down over the escarpment or go NE towards the moor. At a kissing gate, veer right on the broad path, walking downhill. When you emerge on to the lane, with Baslow Edge continuing to the south, you are ready for the final leg, going right, steeply downhill for 1.6 km (one mile) to reach the front of Bridge Inn. The lane is narrow in places, so watch for traffic, and it's from this area that you'll get a view of the mill. It's like any other mill building, I'm afraid, and not a bit like Colditz Castle.

View from Curbar Edge

Walk 20 – River Derwent – Shatton to Leadmill

Along the River Derwent to Leadmill, with the return across high ground overlooking the valley, past Robin Hood's Stoop and Offerton Hall. It's a plain walk with nice views, but with limited additional points of interest. So a look round Hathersage or Castleton would complete the day.

The path by the river is sometimes unfenced, with deep water nearby, so care is needed.

Distance and climb	9.5 km (5.9 miles) and 240m (790 ft), taking about three hours
Grading	Easy, climbing gradient 1 in 12, children need supervision alongside the river
OS map	Landranger 119
Start	Shatton Lane, roadside by the river bridge Shatton is south off the A6187 Hathersage/Hope road, 3 km (two miles) east of hope. The lane is marked as a no-through road, and parking is immediately after the river bridge, 50m off the main road

The walk

There's a stile by the parking spot, with a fingerpost to Leadmill. Take that and follow the path alongside the river – more of the Derwent Valley Heritage Way that is used during Walk 19. It's wooded at first, but soon opens into pasture, with the river always tree-lined, and with numerous streams coming off the high ground to the south, each with a decent footbridge. Most of the time the riverside is well fenced, but some areas are unguarded, with deep water to welcome anyone who slips.

After 1.5 km (a mile) there is a set of stepping-stones. I was

Stepping-stones across the Derwent

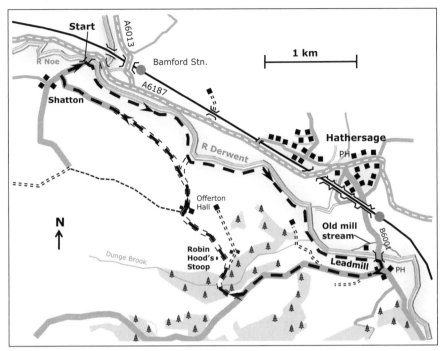

Route map for Walk 20 – River Derwent – Shatton to Leadmill

tempted to send the route across them, just for the challenge, but the path on the other side doesn't go anywhere exciting. So continue on by the water, with a pleasant outlook to the south, which is the return route. Looking south from the stepping-stones, the modest summit beyond the trees is Offerton Moor, which you pass by later. It has an ancient guide post (a 'stoop') – called Robin Hood's Stoop, one of many in Derbyshire. It's alleged to be the place from where Robin Hood shot an arrow into Hathersage Churchyard, about 2.5 km (1.5 miles) away. It's rubbish! The world record for an arrow distance is about 1.9 km, and there is no way an outlaw living in the thirteenth century would have possessed anything other than the most primitive weapon (even assuming he wasn't a myth). I'll bet he couldn't have hit a deer at 200 paces!

Continuing on, the path goes through Goose Nest Wood (I didn't see any) and emerges again into pasture, with Leadmill Bridge in view. 150m before the bridge is the modest weir, with the old millstream leaving from the far bank, now overgrown. The 1881 OS map show the stream clearly, with a corn mill located near where the modern house now stands. It's still there in 1922 and 1955, but gone by 1974. Other than that, I could discover nothing, not even from an old man tending his sheep – 'I lived 'ere all me life,' he admitted. 'But I know newt about it, lad.'

In fact, he had about 100 sheep in a makeshift pen, and was fussing amongs them. I asked if they were going for meat.

'Nay lad. They're goin' t' ram. I were tellin' 'em. Cheer 'em up a bit.'

'What?' I asked, incredulously. 'All those to one ram?'

'Nay lad. More than one. About 30 sheep t' each ram.'

I thought about it for a bit, then asked, 'So how long has he got? To serve his 30 sheep.'

'A fortneet, lad. N' more.'

I did a bit of mental arithmetic.

'That's two every weekday, and three on Sundays,' I concluded. 'I'm impressed!'

He looked back blankly. I think the maths was a step too far.

At the bridge, go right on the B-road; then go right again opposite the Plough Inn, following the lane signposted to the Abney Gliding Club. Then it's uphill for the next 1.5 km (a mile), with the views expanding, and passing under the right flank of Highlow on the way. How can a hill be

Stanage Edge, behind Hathersage

both high and low? 'Low' means 'burial site' of course, so it's the 'high burial ground'.

Just before the Highlow Hall farm on the left, take the lane that forks right, following it down through Dunge Wood and up the other side to pass by the entrance to Callow Farm. (I did reconnoitre an alternative route from Leadmill to the track for Broadhay Farm and on to Callow Farm – see your OS map – but it was muddy, and went downhill just to go uphill again, which I hate.)

The lane swings left from the Callow Farm entrance, below Offerton Moor. (Look out for Robin Hood's Stoop, on the left as you walk, about 10m from the path and surrounded by a rough fence.) It's from there that you get a good view across Hathersage to Stanage Edge (to the north and NE), as well as to Higger Tor (ENE, behind and right of the town). Then behind Higger Tor is Burbage Edge.

You can also appreciate the Derwent valley, stretching away west and then through the gap at Bamford to its exit from Ladybower Reservoir, with Win Hill on the left of the valley and Bamford Edge on the right. The Derwent valley is still 'U'-shaped here, cut by the meandering river, but not as wide as further south, along Walk 19. The river is marked by a continuous line of trees, either side. Why is that? Without man's intervention, for farming, the whole country would be forest, including the entire Derwent valley. So I think the trees by the river escape man's attention, rather than the riverside being particularly favourable for their growth.

The lane turns sharp right and begins to descend steeply. You have an option there to take the path ('Public Bridle Path') across the flank of Offerton Moor (one stream to cross), emerging on to Shatton Lane after 1 km (0.6 mile), where you go right and back to the car. That route is little different in terms of distance and climb, but it can be muddy.

I chose instead to keep on the lane, going past the Offerton Hall farmstead. At the bottom of the hill, where a private track goes right, keep left on the lane, which soon becomes a track, with a gate. That leads on past Garner House, still with good views down to the outward track along the river, eventually becoming a hard lane again and emerging on to Shatton Lane. Go right there, and it's 350m to the car.

Walk 21 – Derwent Reservoir

Under the Derwent dam, alongside the Derwent Reservoir and back across the high ground to the east, dropping down to the Ladybower Reservoir. The final leg is back to the Derwent dam on the east side lane.

Designing a family walk to enjoy the three massive reservoirs on the River Derwent is a challenge. The circular walks around the reservoirs are too long and boring. However, the walk I've selected allows you to see two dams and provides an excellent aerial view of the three reservoirs from the Abbey Bank path, without being too strenuous.

Distance and climb	9.1 km (5.7) miles and 340m (1100 ft), taking about three hours
Grading	Moderate, climbing gradient 1 in 6 (one stiff climb), children friendly
OS map	Landranger 110
Start	Fairholmes car park (pay and display), Ladybower Reservoir Fairholmes is near the Derwent dam, 4 km (2.5 miles) along the lane on the west side of the reservoirs. The lane leaves north from the Ladybower Bridge on the A57 Glossop/Sheffield Snake Road. There are lay-bys (free parking) alongside the lane, the last one after 3 km (two miles)

The walk

The route to the Derwent dam, which is along the lane that leaves right from the roundabout at Fairholmes, is clear no matter where you park. The dam is a formidable structure, with its two turrets and a wide grassy expanse below. Unlike most of the other reservoirs visited during these walks, this dam (and Howden) is meant to overtop. There are no

The Derwent dam from the east turret

spillways or complicated conduits – the water simply flows from Howden into Derwent, then into Ladybower.

If Derwent Reservoir is overtopping, the best place to stand is under the east turret. It's a splendid sight, but wet if the spray is blowing. It was anything but wet when I was there in August 2010, with the water level about 6m below the parapet.

Also by the east turret is a set of steps going down to an underground chamber. That is a sluice, with water tapped off Derwent Reservoir and taken along an underground conduit to the Rivelin reservoirs, a subject discussed more fully in Walk 22.

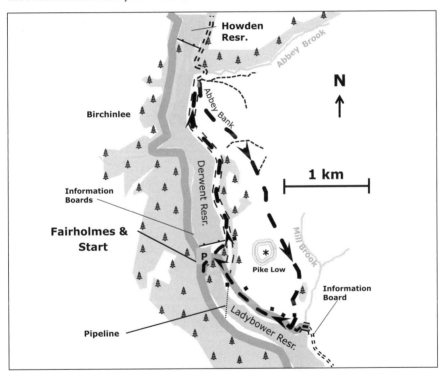

Route Map for Walk 21 – Derwent Reservoir

Walk up the steps by the turret and continue north along the track on the east side. Once clear of the trees, there is a view to the dam and across to the west turret. Close by that turret, a surge of water is pouring in, not from a natural stream, but from an aqueduct that comes from the Alport and Ashop rivers to the west, 3 km (two miles) away. It was an afterthought, when it became clear that the reservoir wasn't filling quickly enough.

Continuing on, I got sight of some old bridge supports, for a railway that once spanned the Ouselden Clough inlet on the west side, exposed by the retreating water. It was a railway line coming from Bamford, bringing in the materials needed to construct the dams. You can learn more about it later.

2.5 km (1.5 miles) on from the Derwent dam, the track begins to swing right, ready to cross Abbey Brook. From the corner, a grass track leaves uphill, signposted as 'Footpath 72'. Take that, and after about 40m (as the sign indicates for Bradfield and Strines) veer right up the steep footpath through the trees. It emerges through a walker's gate, with an Abbey Bank sign close by, where you keep diagonally right, continuing the climb.

The old railway bridge supports, from Abbey Bank

By the time you get to the top, by the trees, there is a good view back to the Howden dam and reservoir. It was built in the early 1900s, along with Derwent, and they both supply water to Derby and Leicester. It arrives at the Midlands towns via a 45 km (28 miles) aqueduct to Ambergate, north of Derby. It gets a mention in Walk 19, where you walk across it on a manhole cover.

The Howden dam and reservoir from Abbey Bank

At the top, follow the path left, indicated to Strines. It crosses a land management track and follows a wall for 400m, before it branches away and crosses a stream, eventually reaching an intersection with other paths. Here, the sign says left to Strines, but you carry straight on to Ashopton, with a nice view of the onward path towards Pike Low.

Along this top path, the views down to the Derwent dam and reservoir are excellent. It's from here that you might best imagine the RAF bombers practising their Dambusters' raids, flying south over the water and between the turrets. (Again, you can learn more about it later.)

Walking on, there's a stile, where you keep straight on. The view to the fore is then across Pike Low to Win Hill, with Lose Hill right and Mam Tor further right. To your left is the Derwent Edge ridge, with the distinctive outcrop of Bamford Edge further south.

There's a sign for Ladybower, one saying 'Footpath', and then another. Keep straight on at these signs, avoiding any side paths (there are many, but the main path is clear). You should be walking generally SE (the sun is due south at midday in winter, or at 1 pm in summer). If you find yourself going SW, you've made a mistake. (Go back.)

Derwent Reservoir and Dam from Abbey Bank

After the second 'Footpath' sign, the path becomes a broader track alongside a ruined wall, going due south to the east side of Pike Low. (Note that, on your 25,000 to 1 OS map, if you have one, this is the dotted track rather than the dashed green path.) It's along this track that you get the first view of Ladybower, with the viaduct carrying the A57. Surprisingly, this massive reservoir is not supplying much drinking water; its main function is to preserve water to maintain the ongoing River Derwent.

With a gate to the fore, the track veers left (SE), downhill, to a stile into open pasture. Then it swings more SW, with a view into the Mill Brook valley on the left, before it reaches Lanehead Farm. The path keeps left of the farm, down an ancient walled track, over a stile, and continues down to the lane alongside Ladybower. From there you will eventually go right, walking back to the Derwent dam and then to the car. (On the way, keep left when the lane forks, near the telephone box.)

Before you do that, make an excursion left, down to the Mill Brook stream inlet to the reservoir, where there is an information board about the drowned village of Derwent. The graves in the Derwent churchyard were moved to Bamford, but the church steeple remained stubbornly above water, until it was deemed unsafe and destroyed. And the old packhorse bridge, which crossed the River Derwent in the village centre, was relocated to the top end of Howden reservoir at Slippery Stones, where it still stands today.

With the reservoir so low, I was able to explore. An old bridge over the incoming Mill Brook was exposed, silted almost to the top. On the 1880 map, that point is shown as a ford; then in 1920 it is the bridge. At that time, the east side lane crossed the stream there, with a Parsonage on the north side. (The gateposts to that are in the trees by the lane corner as you walk back.)

I followed the shoreline back to the pipeline that crosses the reservoir (breaking all the rules). On the way I found many old green and brown bottles, but with no labels to give them some history – pity. Then, near the pipeline, there were some ruins and a network of stones, which looked like the top of old walls, now silted up. On the old maps, the ruin is shown as the 'Water House', with the enclosures nearby.

Exposed bridge, petrified tree stump behind

The silt under the old bridge and the buried enclosure walls got me thinking. How fast do reservoirs silt up? After all, the debris-laden streams come rushing in, joining the placid water. All that debris must then settle out. The answer seems to be a loss of 1% in the capacity every year. That's very significant, meaning that a reservoir can be

Ruin (back right) and enclosures

halved in 50 years unless it is dredged. In a world increasingly short of fresh water, scraping away at the bottom of reservoirs is going to be an urgent requirement.

Continuing with the walk narrative, when you've crossed back over the river after the Derwent dam, instead of going straight back to the car, consider a short excursion to the west tower. There are information boards about the dam and the reservoirs, as well as about the Dambusters. In the turret there is a museum – open Sundays and Bank Holidays. It's well worth a visit, just to see a real size bouncing bomb.

Finally, 500m further north along the west lane there are more information boards about the railway and the labourers' village ('Tin Town', at Birchinlee) that sprung up during the construction phase. Long gone now, but I wonder if the contents of those old bottles I found once fortified some of the workers?

Walk 22 – Rivelin and Redmires Reservoirs

Alongside the Lower Rivelin reservoir, through the Fox Holes Plantation by Wyming Brook, going up to and then around the three Redmires Reservoirs. Return is alongside a conduit, across the Round Hill moor and through the plantation around the Upper Rivelin reservoir.

Distance and climb	9.0 km (5.6 miles) and 210m (700 ft), taking about two and a half hours
Grading	Easy, climbing gradient 1 in 11, children friendly
OS map	Landranger 111
Start	Parking area, south end of Rivelin Lower Reservoir dam The Rivelin reservoirs are alongside the A57 Glossop/Sheffield trunk road, 8 km (five miles) west of Sheffield. The road across the dam is single track with two passing places, priority to arriving vehicles. There is car parking space for about 20 cars

The walk

Follow the track going west on the south side of the lower reservoir for 250m, to where it crosses Wyming Brook. Then take the public footpath through the nature reserve, alongside the brook. It's very picturesque, but tricky in places, with waterfalls, bridges and stepping stones, and will usually be slippery. The brook takes water from Lower Redmires Reservoir down to Lower Rivelin Reservoir, the name 'Wyming' being from the Dutch, meaning 'riverbed'. It predates all the reservoirs (mid 19th century), of course, originally rising from Rud Hill, south of the Redmires.

The path emerges on to a car park. Go left, on to the Redmires

Scene along Wyming Brook

Road lane, where you go left again, walk 200m up the hill and turn right, down Soughley Lane. After 150m there is a public footpath to the right, along a walled track. Beneath it is the Redmires Conduit, part of the drainage system to shepherd water into the reservoirs, all explained in the water-flow diagram later in this narrative.

Don't follow that path; keep on the lane for another 200m, to the corner, and then take the stile on the right, following the path on to Water Board property. At the wall corner (150m), go left; then take the kissing gate to the right, alongside the SE corner of the lower reservoir. All the outlets for this reservoir are on the north side, with the valve tower visible at the dam centre and a spillway in the NW corner for overflow conditions, the water going through filters before it rushes down Wyming Brook.

'Redmire' means 'pool covered with reeds', and I can imagine the area being very marshy before the reservoirs were built. But the new path around the south of the water is relatively dry and easy to follow. It keeps

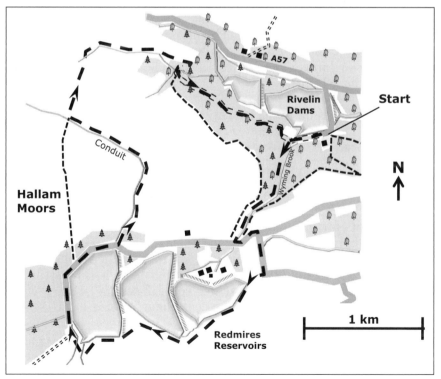

Route Map for Walk 22 – Rivelin and Redmires Reservoirs

Upper Redmires Reservoir

close to the lower reservoir at first, turns uphill to the south end of the middle dam and then follows a conduit running parallel with the water's edge. That conduit captures the water coming off Rud Hill (Wyming Brook again), the original stream course having been interrupted by the lower reservoir.

Cross the conduit on the wooden bridge and follow the path (muddy in places) to the south end of the upper dam. From there the path soon turns south, away from the water, looping round to cross the various cloughs that feed the SW corner of the upper reservoir. Before that loop is a small hillock on the left, with a photo opportunity to capture all three reservoirs.

The path emerges on to the lane at the west end of the reservoirs. Go right there and follow it round to the NE corner of the upper reservoir, where you go left by the information board, up the 'easy cycle' route. That path follows a conduit, constructed to capture as much water as possible from the moors. It weirs into the upper reservoir, but there is a bell-mouth overflow for flooding conditions, taking excess water to the lower reservoirs, or even direct to the Wyming Brook (see the water-flow map).

The conduit path goes north and then NW, with good views down to Sheffield and across the moors to the north, and NW towards Stanage Edge. There are two farmer's access bridges, an anonymous folly (a plain stone tower) and then a third bridge at a crossing path. Go right there, down across the moor. In the distance you can see the solitary 'Head Stone' rock pillar, and the high ground on the other side of the Rivelin Valley is Rod Moor.

After 400m there is a stream; then 100m on from that is a marker post. Go right there and follow the narrow path through the heather. It keeps to the higher ground, with stream valleys either side, and reaches a kissing gate through a boundary fence. To the right of that, lower down, is another path, with an identical kissing gate. I missed the fork off the top path to that one, and in retrospect, that lower path might be better. I suggest you try it.

I kept on the higher path, fighting my way through the ferns and into the wooded area, where it got rather vague. Whichever path you take, it concludes with a tricky descent through the trees on to the track called Wyming Brook Drive, where you go right. That loops back SE, above the upper Rivelin Reservoir, which is mostly hidden by the trees. Further on, when the track forks, keep left, downhill, and you will soon reach the Wyming Brook again.

On the left at that point there is a grassy clearing, with an ornate stone arch and protective grill. I peered in, to see a sinister tunnel disappearing into the darkness, with the sound of falling water. The clearing is the top of a collection tank, and the tunnel comes from the east turret of the Derwent dam, 8km (five miles) away. In 1903, the mill owners below the Rivelin dams were demanding extra flow, and to drain more of the precious Sheffield drinking water from the Redmires was considered unsatisfactory. Derwent had plenty, they said, so the tunnel was built to

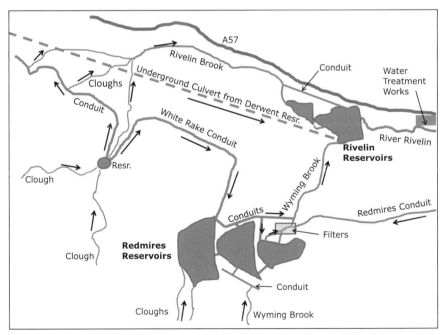

Water flow map for Rivelins and Redmires Reservoirs

Lower Rivelin Reservoir

steal it. The fall over the 8 km is only 2m, so the gradient is a gentle 1 in 4000.

It's worth looking into the arch, if you don't mind hopping over the gate; then it's just 250m back to the car and a chance to get a good picture.

Finally, to complete the details on the reservoirs, the Redmires collect their water off Rud Hill to the south and from the SE portion of Hallam Moor to the west, with only a 20 to 1 catchment ratio (see the 50:1 OS maps). The Rivelins take water from the NW portion of Hallam Moor, with a 40 to 1 catchment. If you study the water flow map above, you can see how the little reservoir at the centre of the conduit can be used to direct water to either reservoir group, depending on the need.

Walk 23 – Dale Dike and Strines Reservoirs

An easy circuit of Dale Dike Reservoir, first walking along the SE side of the water, with an option to make an excursion to visit the 'Boot's Folly' tower. After viewing the Strines dam, return is on a higher track via Hallfield. It's possible to walk back along the NW edge of the reservoir, but the Hallfield track adds some variety, with wider views and less woodland walking.

There are two more walks close by (combined into Walk 24), starting from Low Bradfield, both easy. You might squeeze all three into one day.

Distance and climb	**5.4 km (3.4 miles) and 140m (470 ft), taking about 1.5 hours, or 7.0 km (4.4 miles) and 230m (750 ft) if you visit Boot's Folly, taking about 2.5 hours**
Grading	**Easy, climbing gradient 1 in 16, (1 in 13 when including Boot's Folly), children friendly**
OS map	**Landranger 110**
Start	**Lay-by, Dale Road, Thornseat, next to the Dale Dike entrance, with room for five cars** **Thornseat is 2 km (1.2 miles) west of Low Bradfield, itself 8 km (five miles) NW from Sheffield on the B6077. I approached from the A57, east of Ladybower, following the lane north (Mortimer Road) signposted to Strines Moor. It passes 'The Strines' pub, goes round an inlet and then between two plantations. Dale Road is the first right, at the end of the plantations**

The walk

Take the stile by the gate, with the public footpath marker, and follow the track towards the Dale Dike dam. It's not long before you pass a small memorial to the 1864 Dale Dike disaster, and as far as I could see there were no other information boards to elaborate. Apparently, the dam burst whilst they were first filling the reservoir, and the subsequent flood that surged down the River Loxley killed 270 people on its way to, and then through, Sheffield. Surprisingly, it still ranks in the top twenty flood disasters of all time, worldwide. On its way, the water demolished the

Dale Dike Reservoir from the east end of the dam

village of Damflask, so they were saved a job when they later came to build the Damflask reservoir (Walk 24).

Walking on, the track divides. The walk route goes left, downhill, but first follow the onward track for 150m to the north corner of the reservoir, where there is probably the best view. A path continues on the

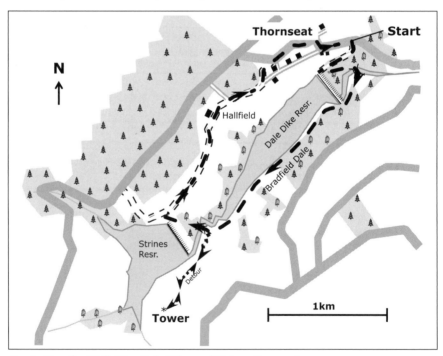

Route Map for Walk 23 – Dale Dike and Strines Reservoirs

NW side of the water from there, but we're not going that way. Also, a notice discourages you from walking across the grass-topped dam, but I did so anyway (looking for better pictures). At the other end, where the walk route passes by again, there was a gate that was easy to climb, with a footbridge over the dam spillway – but I'm not advocating such a route.

Having viewed the dam, return to the fork and go downhill. The track meanders down to a bridge over the outgoing stream ('Dale Dike' – which goes on to feed Damflask Reservoir), with a small pool (made by the small 'Deversoir Dam') and a valve house and sluice to control the outflow. There is no valve tower up by the dam, as with most reservoirs.

The path continues up steps on the other side and passes by the east corner of the reservoir, as I mentioned above. In September 2010, the spillway was bone dry and overgrown, and the ducks were touching the bottom with their feet. From there, follow the SE side of the water, passing the old pump house on the way to the SW limit of the reservoir, ignoring any paths that leave left on the way. It's easy walking, except for the tree roots, with frequent views across the water.

At the SW end the path emerges briefly from the trees and swings right, the ongoing route. There is a marker post there (green and yellow arrows) and a path going back left. That is the way to the Folly, if you are so minded, and I've described that leg at the end of this narrative.

Continuing from the post on the main walk, going right, the path quickly divides. Right again would take you along the NW side of the reservoir, back to the Dale Dike dam, and you would miss the Strines reservoir. Left is the route, over a footbridge, through the trees and up to the NW corner of the Strines dam.

This reservoir dates to 1869, along with the other three nearby, providing water to Sheffield (but it was 1875 before Dale Dike was rebuilt, after the breach). You are again discouraged from walking across the dam,

Strines Reservoir from near Boot's Folly

with the valve house and spillway at the other end, taking the water into Dale Dike. My best picture was from up near Boot's Folly, but I can confirm that there is no way of sneaking across the dam and up the other side to reach that tower.

To return, take the track that goes NE from the reservoir corner, below the plantation, past Stubbing Farm. There are a couple of gates, and it crosses pastureland, with nice views down to Dale Dike and backwards towards the tower. At Hallfield there is a concession path to take you round the posh house, rejoining the track on the other side, skirting more plantations. As you approach Thompson House Farm, with a 'No Footpath' sign to the fore, veer left, through the gate and up the narrower grass track. It emerges on to Dale Road, where you go right and walk back 800m (half a mile) to the car.

Route to Boot's Folly

From the marker post, take the path over the wall stile and then walk 50m straight up the grassy slope to intercept the crossing 'Sheffield Country Walk' path. Go right and follow it uphill, with the tower in view. It's about 1 km (half a mile), and it was muddy, even after such a dry spell in 2010. Then you retrace this route to go back to the main walk.

The Folly was built in 1927 by Charles Boot, the owner of Sugworth Hall. It was the usual story of giving his workers something to do during the Great Depression.

You can't climb up it, which is a shame, because they've removed the spiral staircase. That was the fault of a cow, which became stuck trying to climb the steps. I have a vision of about six farmhands trying to prise the cow lose and persuade it to backup down the stairs.

Boot's Folly – jealously guarded

When I arrived it was surrounded by more cows, all giving me menacing looks, so there was no way I was going to approach it. (I hate cows!) I think they might even take shelter in it. But the views were good, particularly over the Strines reservoir, so the excursion was just about worth the effort.

Walk 24 – Agden and Damflask Reservoirs

The walk is divided into two, around each reservoir in turn, coming back to Low Bradfield at the halfway point. Both are easy to follow, close to the water for the majority of the route.

Low Bradfield is very popular. They've gone out of their way to cater for walkers, with numbered routes going in all directions. The village green, cricket pitch, pavilion and bowling green provide the classic English scene. It's paid off, because it was heaving with people when I got there in early September 2010, with picnic areas, ice cream, pubs, coffee shops and family groups relaxing on the green. (I once visited on a cold and frosty January morning. They were playing cricket and holding a mediaeval jousting competition on the green! I was impressed.)

Distance and climb	1 Agden: 4 km (2.5 miles) and 80m (260 ft), taking about one hour 2 Damflask: 5.7 km (3.5 miles) and 60m (200 ft), taking about 1.5 hours
Grading	Both easy, climbing gradient 1 in 25, children friendly except for one part of the Agden walk, where there is an alternative route
OS map	Landranger 110
Start	Low Bradfield village centre – Smithy Bridge Road Low Bradfield is 8 km (five miles) NW from Sheffield on the B6077. I approached from the A57, east of Ladybower, following the lane north (Mortimer Road) signposted to Strines Moor. It passes 'The Strines' pub, goes round an inlet and then between two plantations. The first turn right, at the end of the plantations, leads down to Low Bradfield, via Dale Road, Annet Lane and Fair House Lane, from which you turn left into the village centre

The walks

Part 1 – Agden Reservoir
If you've already completed Walk 23, you'll have seen Strines and Dale Dike Reservoirs. With Agden and Damflask, they make a group of four

constructed to provide water for Sheffield, drawing on the many streams and dikes coming off the extensive Bradfield and Ughill Moors. 'Agden' means either 'sheep pasture' or 'oak valley' - whichever, it was drowned by the reservoir. 'Damflask' is more difficult. It probably comes from 'Danslaske' - a local route or 'intake' where fodder could be taken to grazing stock.

The four reservoirs were built in the late 1800s, linked together to supply water treatment works in NW Sheffield. Together, they collect water from 4000 hectares of moor, that's 33 times their combined surface area. The map shows how the water flow works, with Damflask Reservoir also fulfilling the role of maintaining a reliable flow down the River Loxley, on its way to the River Don. It was the usual story of keeping the mills turning, even during long dry spells.

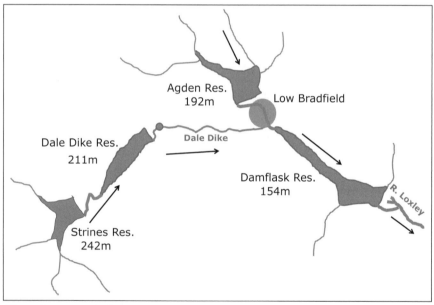

Water flow map for four reservoirs

To start the walk, follow 'The Sands' lane that leaves from the bend in the lane going up to Higher Bradfield, past the village hall. Take the footpath to the right marked as No 35 and follow it to the footbridge over the dam spillway. Don't cross it; go right up the steps instead, following the path between a wall and a fence, emerging on to Smallfield Lane, where you go left.

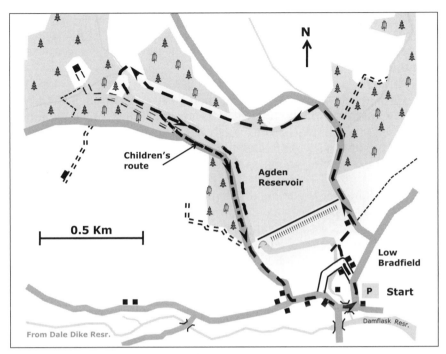

Route Map for Walk 24, Part 1 – Agden Reservoir

It's about 150m to the dam. I disobeyed the notice by shinning over the wall and walking to the other end, where I got some good photographs across the water towards Rocher Edge to the north. Standing on the top of the dam and looking down, I couldn't help wondering what would become of Low Bradfield if it burst. It would be devastated – plain and simple. The water would surge through the village, carrying all before it, and then go on to fill up Damflask, which would soon overtop its dam. Once overtopped, that dam would be rapidly eroded, and Sheffield would then be at the water's mercy.

Walking on along Smallfield Lane, it's 500m to the start of the reservoir concessionary walk. It

Agden Reservoir – from the start of the concession path

follows the tree-line by the edge of the water, with a view across to the dam. After turning west, a marker post directs the path to the right, up to a track, where you go left and follow it to the limit of the reservoir, with the Agden Beck stream on the left.

Go left at the post with the green arrow, across the footbridge, along the wall, through the walker's gate, and then steeply up through the trees. Half way up, follow the path to the left, now quite high above the water. Ultimately, this path reaches the 'Windy Bank' lane at the top, intersecting a track at its exit. (The track is behind the wall, above you.) That way is best if you have young children, then walking on down the lane towards the dam.

To walk nearer the water, about 100m before the path reaches the track, look for a vague path leaving left, down the slope. It's marked by a lying tree trunk, braced with ground posts. That path has several spots where there is a big, unprotected drop into the water – not a place for youngsters, particularly if it's wet.

Finally, you emerge on to Windy Bank Lane just before the west end of the reservoir, with a property nearby. That used to be the 'Keeper's House', a man who looked after the dam. Presumably, he walked it before his breakfast, again before lunch, then after tea, and filed his report at the end of the day – 'Dam remains intact – such and such date'. Sounds like a good job to me.

From there it's downhill past the dam spillway, which hadn't seen a drop of water for months when I visited, to Fair House Lane, where you turn left back to the village.

Part 2 – Damflask Reservoir

From Smithy Bridge Road, walk past the garage and down the lane (Lamb Hill) signposted to Loxley. After 60m, go right down the track, over the bridge and then immediately left on to the reservoir path ('Yorkshire Water Permissive Path').

It's nicely made, leading close by the in-flowing stream and then the widening reservoir, before it enters the wooded area alongside the water. There are pleasant views across to the other side, and there may be sailing boats to

Damflask Reservoir – towards the dam

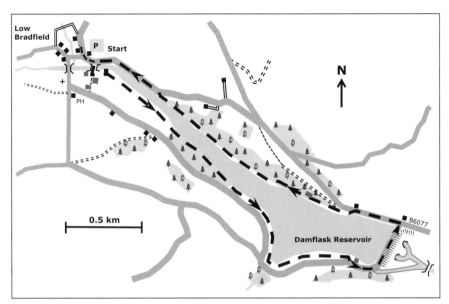

Route Map for Walk 24, Part 2 – Damflask Reservoir)

watch. The path eventually runs close to the roadside, emerging on to New Road just before the old Keeper's Lodge, now a private residence.

You must cross the dam using New Road. The spillway is in the SE corner, dry when I visited; then the two valve towers meter the water to the double outlet below the dam (see the water sketch). If you stand at the centre of the dam and look out across the water, the old village of Damflask would have been below you. There was a paper mill, a corn mill and 'Mill House', confirming again how important the waterpower was to the area.

A lane ('Flash Hill') linked New Road with Loxley Road on the north side of the reservoir, so its remnants must still be down there. And you turn down Loxley Road to continue the walk, walking for 200m on the pavement before re-entering the reservoir area and picking up the concession path. There is the boating area and some seats with a pleasant outlook over the water, before you eventually emerge back on to the Lamb Hill lane, with 500m back to Low Bradfield.

Walk 25 – Langsett Reservoir

Clockwise around the reservoir, crossing the dam, using a concessionary path through the Midhope plantation, a high level moor path with good views, and then a waterside return path on the north side. There is a permissive path that keeps to the water's edge on the south side, but I much preferred the higher ground and a break from the forest walking.

Distance and climb	5.8 km (3.6 miles) and 180m (600 ft), taking about two hours
Grading	Easy, climbing gradient 1 in 12, children friendly
OS map	Landranger 110
Start	Langsett Barn car park, Langsett Langsett is on the A616 trunk road joining the M1 and the A628 Woodhead Pass, 2 km (1.5 miles) SE of the A628 roundabout. A large car park is 200m east of the village centre. Langsett Barn refers to a 17th century lodge, now used as the ranger station and visitor centre

The walk

Langsett means 'the long slope', where sheep would be led to pasture in summer, and the 1895 map, just before the reservoir was built, shows a line of south-facing enclosures between what is now the main road and the then course of the River Don. So, unlike some of the reservoirs, this one didn't drown any villages, just farming country.

Leave the car park towards the water, down the slope, going left where the path divides and following it to Midhope Cliff Lane and the dam. In late October 2010, even after much needed rain, the reservoir was low and the spillway in the NE corner was bone dry. Unlike some of the reservoirs, this one is straightforward – no complex conduits or leats; just a simple pool of water.

The valve tower is ornate, metering the water to the treatment works below the dam, and then onwards to Sheffield. I tried in vain to interpret the Latin inscription on the tower – I think it describes the date when the reservoir was constructed.

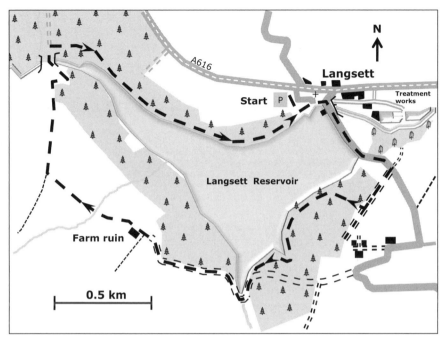

Route Map for Walk 25 – Langsett Reservoir

Having crossed the dam, follow the lane as it bends left and right; then take the track (Joseph Lane) to the right, at the edge of the trees. After 250m go right into the wood on the 'Permissive Path', keeping right at the next marker post to walk close to the water. The trees open out, with a small inlet, and then a larger inlet (Thickwoods Brook) where you join a forest track (Thickwoods Lane), turning back on the other side after a bridge and a weir. I got my best photograph from that area.

Follow the track uphill, above the tree line, to a gate, with the heather moor beyond. They were harvesting the trees when I was there, with the view down to the reservoir being opened out. So I'm optimistic that, when you read this

Walking through the plantation

Langsett Reservoir from the south

book, it will all be completed. Looking at the moors to the south and SW, the main catchment area is 2000 hectares (20 sq km), and the reservoir area is 50 hectares; so that's 40 to 1, similar to other reservoirs in the Peak District.

After the gate there is a ruin. It is the remains of 'The North America Farm', pulled down when the reservoir was built (to reduce pollution from farming activities). Its name goes back to the time of the British Empire, when farmers liked to celebrate our far-flung colonies – 'Quebec Farm' was another example. Have a look at the stones; you might find some pot-marks from army target practise, before the D-Day landings.

At the high point, the track reaches a crossing path (Cut Gate Track). Go right, following it down to the trees, around the contours, and across the Little Don river (also called 'The Porter') on the old Brookhouse Bridge. There's a 50m steep climb on the other side before you turn right at the fingerpost and follow the well-made path through the trees. It quickly divides – keep right, down to the wall alongside the incoming river, where you follow the path back to the start, with several seats to enjoy the outlook over the water.

Walk 26 – Kinder Reservoir

This is an easy circuit of the reservoir, in a lasso-shaped walk, clockwise. Outward is on the east side to the bottom of William Clough. Inward is around the west side via Upper House and Farlands Booth.

Distance and climb	7 km (4.4 miles) and 250m (850 ft), taking about 2.5 hours
Grading	Easy, climbing gradient 1 in 16, children friendly
OS map	Landranger 110
Start	Bowden Bridge car park (pay and display), Kinder Road Kinder Road leaves SE off Market Street in Hayfield village, on the A624 Glossop/Chapel-en-le-Frith road. It's then 1.5 km (one mile) to the car park, with additional parking roadside to avoid the charge

The walk

Before leaving the car park, read the commemorative plaque on the rock face at the back, and the poem on the seat. They mark an important event, the 'Mass Trespass', one that paved the way for the walking privileges that we enjoy today. Hundreds of ramblers set off for the Kinder plateau, determined to walk over the private land. Their point was that any person should be allowed to enjoy the beauty of the hills and moors without threat of prosecution from the landowners.

The gentry's response was predictable. They couldn't have all those oiks trampling over their grouse moor and spoiling their bag, so they recruited extra gamekeepers, with several fights ensuing. Prosecutions followed, but the door had been prised open – now we have 'Right to Roam' over large areas of land.

Booth Sheepwash

To start the walk, leave the car park and follow Kinder Road, signposted to Kinder Scout via William Clough. After 1 km (0.6 mile), the road reaches a gate marking the entrance to Water Board property, with the remains of the old Booth Sheepwash on the right. Read the information board – somehow, I don't think their sheep dip would comply with today's European regulations!

You can either carry on through the gates ('Concession bridleway to Kinder Reservoir', as on the route map), or go right up the lane (the return route of the walk) and then left through the gate to walk alongside the river, crossing back on a footbridge after 250m. Either way, you reach the locked gates to the reservoir, where the route goes through the walker's gate on the left and follows the cobbled path. It's an old donkey track, the cobbles giving the animals extra grip.

As you gain height, look over the wall at the dam and the derelict water treatment works below. Nowadays, the water is treated nearer the customer – Stockport – and I've never seen any activity under the dam. It was built in 1911, and claimed the title of largest earth dam in the world, a record it must have lost a thousand times over since then.

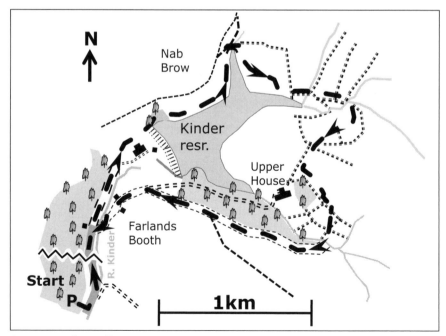

Route Map for Walk 26 – Kinder Reservoir

Kinder Reservoir – February 2010

You can see the spillway coming down from the south side, and the valve tower on the north side. Below the dam is a flow-monitoring point and a sampling area. In 2010 there was no water coming down the spillway for at least the first ten months of the year.

The path leads to a walker's gate and then runs alongside the reservoir, with good views back towards the dam and forward across the water to the Kinder plateau. To the south are Mount Famine and South Head. I got my best picture from higher up, on Middle Moor, but this walk does not venture up there.

From the reservoir side you can appreciate the bowl-shaped catchment area, which also includes the flat top of the Kinder plateau. The sketch shows how it works, with dozens of streams (I've drawn just a few) channelling water from the high ground. The main source is the River Kinder, reaching back across the peat bogs on the top for about 1 km ('Kinder Gates'); then tumbling over the 'Downfall'. That river is only 5 km long (three miles), emerging below the dam and joining the River Sett near the Bowden Bridge car park.

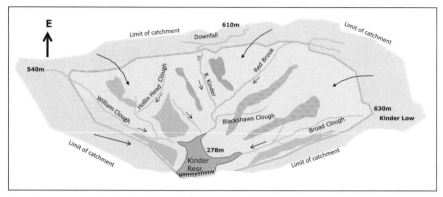

Catchment map for Kinder Reservoir

The reservoir area is about 20 hectares, with a catchment of about 1000 hectares. So that's 50 to 1. Does that mean that 1 cm (half an inch) of rain over the catchment will raise the reservoir by 50 cm (nearly 2 ft)? I don't think so – the vegetation will collect a lot, with losses from evaporation and transpiration.

To complete the walk, cross the footbridge at the end of the William Clough inlet and then turn back on the other side. (It's a narrow path close to the water, not the broader path that strikes off uphill towards the Kinder top.) It loops round, leaving the water's edge, to reach a stile, where you keep right (downhill) as a faint grass path leaves to the left.

Having crossed a small stream, there is then a stile over a wall to the fore. Do not take that – keep left and follow the left side of the onward wall down to a footbridge over the River Kinder. On the other side, the track swings back right, eventually following the left side of a wall. At a fingerpost, go left, following the path around the left side of a wooded enclosure. As you clear the trees, with the track veering left, keep right on the narrower grass track, down to a walker's gate.

On the other side, head downhill, aiming for the left of the wooded area, where you have to ford Broad Clough. It's not difficult, but when the river is in flood, explore upstream for a spot where you can jump it. On the other side, go right over the stile and follow the edge of the trees, eventually emerging on to a lane via a gate. Go left there, following the road back to Kinder Lane to rejoin the outward route.

I had hoped to detour right from the gate, to get another view of the reservoir and spillway, but access is forbidden I'm afraid.

Walk 27 – Torside Reservoir and Crowden

Across the main road to a concession path, going west to the Torside dam; then coming back on a track following a disused railway. The final leg is under the Woodhead dam and back to the concession path. The only significant hazard is crossing the main road.

Distance and climb	6.9 km (4.3 miles) and 170m (540 ft), taking about two hours
Grading	Easy, climbing gradient 1 in 15, children friendly
OS map	Landranger 110
Start	**Crowden car park** Crowden is on the A628 Manchester/Sheffield road, 10 km (six miles) NE of the M67 terminus, with Torside Reservoir opposite. The parking facility, which was free, is clearly signposted from both directions

The walk

Leave the car park westwards, past an information board to the toilet block. Then go left to the main road, left again for about 30m, and cross to the concession path. It goes south, to the reservoir inlet area, with a fingerpost after 50m indicating left to the Woodhead dam (the return leg), and onwards to the Torside dam. The path curves right and joins what used to be a railway ('Dismantled Railway' on the OS maps), taking you across the incoming Crowden Brook. I'm sure this railway was used to service the construction phase (dating to around 1850), since it runs along the entire chain of the five Longendale reservoirs.

The path is soon joined by a channel from the right, coming under the main road. It's a conduit, tapped off the Crowden Brook near the Crowden parking area, running to the Torside dam. It's part of a complex water system, a lot of which I couldn't understand. But I've drawn a map anyway. (I refer to it again later.)

The path runs between the conduit and the reservoir for 1 km (half a mile), then crosses the channel on a footbridge and enters woodland.

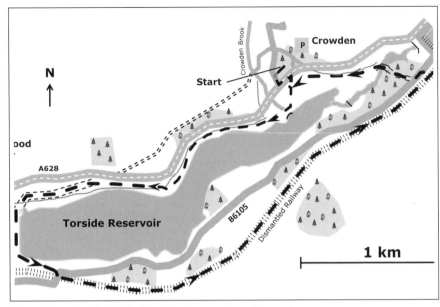

Route Map for Walk 27 – Torside Reservoir and Crowden

There are some open areas, with views of the water, before you join the Pennine Way (which comes down from the main road). Follow that west, with more pleasant woodland, before you go left through a gate and down some steps to the Torside dam, crossing the conduit again on the way, as well as the dam spillway. If you look east along the conduit you'll see a

Rhodeswood Reservoir from the Torside dam – at low ebb

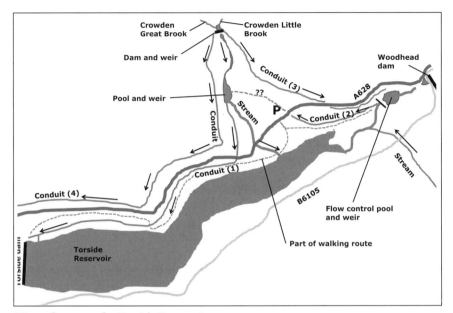

Water flow map for Torside Reservoir

weir and sluice, giving the Water Authority the option of taking the flow into Torside or letting it go on to the lower reservoirs. It's clearly a means of dividing the large flow that comes through Crowden between the reservoirs, as the levels dictate.

At the dam you overlook Rhodeswood Reservoir, and later in the walk you'll pass under the Woodhead dam defending the top reservoir in the chain. Between them, Woodhead (elevation 238m), Torside (196m) and Rhodeswood (176m) satisfy most of Greater Manchester's water needs, channelling the flow into Arnfield Reservoir (162m). That's just west of Tintwistle, where the main water treatment works is situated, and the water then goes on to Godley Reservoir (near Hyde, 141m) via the Mottram Tunnel, ready for distribution. The catchment area is huge, with water coming off the Bleaklow and Howden moors to the south, as well as the extensive moors to the north, all for one city.

Below Rhodeswood are two more reservoirs, Valehouse (157m) and Bottoms (also 157m), completing the chain of five along the valley. But these are not providing drinking water (they are lower than Arnfield). Predictably, they were built to keep the River Etherow flowing for the all-powerful mill owners.

Torside Reservoir from the dam – depleted

Walking on from the dam, you reach the B6105. To cross it, go right, then left, and on the other side follow the fingerpost directions to 'Trans-Pennine Trail East' (not the track higher up, which is the Pennine Way going up to Bleaklow). The path then forks – select the one for walker's and cyclists. It's then 2.5 km (1.5 miles) on the limestone track that was once the route of the Woodhead Railway, running between Manchester and Sheffield, the 'Longendale Trail', just one section of the Trans-Pennine Trail that goes from Liverpool to Hull. At the halfway point there is a path down to the Torside Visitor's Centre, with information boards and refreshments.

I did this walk on Sunday August 15th 2010, on a beautiful day. In one ear I had the sound of hundreds of grouse being massacred on the Bleaklow hillside, and in the other was the roar of motorcycles burning up the B6105 and on to the Woodhead Pass. Later, near the reservoir, I was assaulted by swarms of flying ants. I suggest you do this walk in the autumn, on a weekday!

As you near the Woodhead dam, the B6105 runs alongside the path. 200m before the bend in the road as it crosses the dam, look for a path going back west to a gate on to the road (under the pylons), where you cross to a track through the trees on the other side. That takes you down to a water catchment area under the Woodhead spillway, with a footbridge over the weir.

It was empty in August 2010, but its function is clear. It arrests the flow as it pours off Woodhead, then lets it proceed more gently over the weir, minimising erosion of the wildlife area that's downstream, before Torside.

On the north side of the weir is a sluice, controlling water into another conduit (No 2 on the water flow map), one that you follow on final leg back to the car. On the way there is a bridge, with a signpost to Crowden car park. Don't follow that one; it results in extra road walking. Carry on to the outgoing path at the fingerpost.

Flow control area, off the Woodhead dam

The conduit's function puzzled me. I had expected it to loop round Torside as an emergency bypass into Rhodeswood, but it actually swings NW to disappear under the main road and Crowden car park. You can see from the question marks on my water flow map that I wasn't sure where it then goes – possibly to the 'weir and pool' in Crowden Brook, where there would be the option of sending some of the water on to Rhodeswood via conduit No 1.

Before returning to the car, you could carry on north past the toilet block and follow the road on from the gate towards the education centre. The road soon curves left, over a bridge, but you should go straight on off the bend and follow the track up to a bridge over a yet another conduit (No 3 on the flow map), with the Brockhurst Nature Reserve to the fore. Go through the gate on the left of the conduit, where you can follow it to the Crowden Weir.

It's a curious spot, dividing the water into three, some down the river to Torside (to subsequently divide again, as I mentioned earlier) and the two conduits leave either side. The west conduit (No 4) goes to Rhodeswood, north of the main road for most of its route. But, as you can see from the water map, the east conduit (No 3) passes under the main road, and carries on towards the flow control pool under the Torside dam. Does it flow into it? One of these days I'll go back and work it all out properly.

Walk 28 – Dove Stone, Yeoman Hey and Greenfield Reservoirs

Alongside the NW side of the three reservoirs, turning back across the Greenfield dam and returning on the SE side. There is the option of going around Greenfield (fording a stream) and another option of walking up to the Birchen Clough gully to view some additional water features.

Distance and climb	6.9 km (4.3 miles) and 210m (700 ft), taking about two hours, or up to 9.1 km (5.7 miles) and 290m (950ft – three hours) if you go a bit further
Grading	Easy, climbing gradient 1 in 14, children friendly
OS map	Landranger 109
Start	Dam car park at Dove Stone Reservoir Dove Stone is off the A635 Stalybridge/Holmfirth road, just south of Tunstead. The lane going to the reservoir is clearly signposted – an easy right filter when going NE, but a sharp turn back left when coming downhill, SE. Parking is under the dam, with extensive facilities, and very popular. The modest charge is unavoidable

The walk

The three reservoirs are a fascinating study on how a water supply system is managed, as well as being a hugely popular walk, with a dramatic backdrop of rocky outcrops and hills. To help, I've shown the water plan first, so you'll need to refer to that as you walk around.

From the car park, go up to the dam wall and follow it north, with pleasant views across the water to the Dean and Ashway outcrops. On a poor day for light, I got my best picture of the depleted reservoir from the south, with insufficient water for the sailing boats; even after July 2010 had contributed some much needed rain.

At the north end of the dam there is the overspill and valve-house. It's a bell-mouth design, and makes a splendid sight when the reservoir is overfull. The output from that is low down, into the ongoing Chew Brook, and the valve system must allow a continuous output (hidden) to maintain

Dove Stone Reservoir from the south – Alderman's Hill on the left

the river, as well as providing drinking water for a treatment works
further down the valley.

With two mills (Greenfield and Waterside) under the dam, they were
cautious about the spillway system, with an innovative mechanical 'fuse'
at a level just above that of the bell-mouth. In truly exceptional rainfall

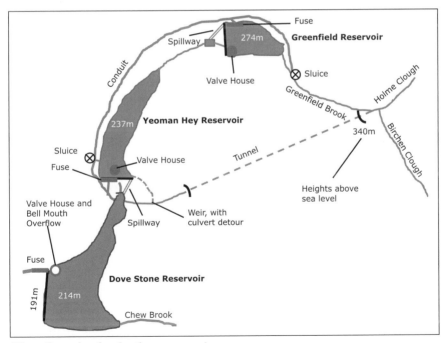

Water flow plan for the three reservoirs

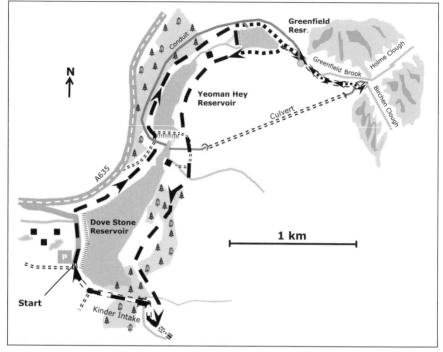

Route Map for Walk 28 – Dove Stone, Yeoman Hey and Greenfield Reservoirs

conditions, with the bell-mouth not coping and the dam wall threatened with overtopping, the metal gates (visible over the concrete wall) will tip, decanting a deluge of water. It would cross the road (closed by then!) and flow directly into the river. There are more 'fuses' on the higher dams.

From the dam, follow the wide path alongside the reservoir, keeping close to the water. As you reach the SW corner of the Yeoman Hey dam there are two features to note – the triple spillway coming down to a channel that feeds into the on-going stream below the dam, and that channel itself, flowing from the west side of the reservoir. It's a conduit, bringing water in a bypass around both the upper dams.

As you walk to the top you'll see a sluice and weir in the conduit on the left, allowing water to be diverted into the Yeoman Hey reservoir, should it be required. And if you look at the top of the triple spillway there are the massive concrete blocks (the 'fuse') that would topple if the normal spillway on the east side of the dam failed to cope with a flood.

Greenfield Reservoir from the east – very low (Early August 2010)

Walking on, following the NW side of Yeoman Hey, keep to the wide track, with trees coming between you and the water before the Greenfield dam comes into view. The path crosses the conduit, and goes to the NW corner of the dam, where the water system is so complex that I'm not sure I fully understood it.

There is a normal spillway coming down from the corner to skim off excess water when the reservoir is full, and the conduit that goes down alongside Yeoman Hey appears out of the dam face. Next to the top of the spillway is another emergency 'fuse' of massive concrete blocks which, if they tipped, would dump the water into a narrow channel (against the wall; you need to lean over), which I suspect then runs out along the conduit from the dam face. Beyond that, a higher section of conduit coming from the top of Greenfield cascades water into a huge square pit, which I think goes on to join the outgoing conduit. Finally, if you look along the dam to the other end, there is the valve-house, with a modest channel of continuous water appearing from near the base of the dam, always feeding into Yeoman Hey.

I stood back and considered it all. The object is to stop the dam overtopping – that would be disastrous. Looking at the spillway, it's hard to imagine so much water coming down from the hills that the spillway couldn't let it all out quickly enough. But someone must have done the calculation, so that if the fuse tips over, probably twice as much water would be emptying. Goodness knows how the conduit would cope downstream.

Having been bemused by all that, you can now cross the dam and turn back downstream on the other side, taking the gate and narrow path that leads down close to the Yeoman Hey water. Or you could carry on and circle Greenfield Reservoir, coming back to the south end of the dam on the other side. However, that means fording the incoming Greenfield Brook at the top (there are some rough stepping stones, just before the sluice where the conduit is fed off from the brook) and using a difficult narrow path along the south edge of the reservoir. None of that is children friendly.

Birchen Clough tunnel

A third, preferred, option is to carry on beyond the top of Greenfield to the confluence of Holme Clough and Birchen Clough (a 800m walk). Here, there is yet more complex water management, with a tunnel leading away south-westwards. Back in 1880 when the two upper reservoirs were built, the mill owners down in the valley were incensed, claiming the lakes would hoard all the water and dry up Chew Brook, the money earning millwheels then grinding to a halt. So the tunnel was built to guarantee a flow, taking water directly to the base of Yeoman Hey. You'll see the exit later – it's a straight 1.4 km run (nearly a mile).

An arresting army

Now, of course, with the mill era gone and Dove Stone Reservoir added on at the bottom (1960s), the tunnel water no longer contributes directly to the ongoing brook.

Assuming you then retrace your steps and cross the Greenfield dam, the path on the east side runs to the east corner of the Yeoman Hey dam. Now you can look down the spillway, with its army of posts. They are to moderate the flow, reducing erosion at the bottom

Yeoman Hey Reservoir from the SE corner – Alderman's Hill behind

From there, continue on the wide path, dropping down to cross a bridge over yet another channel, with water coming down a staircase of weirs. This is the outlet (further up the hill) from the Birchen Clough tunnel, augmented by natural streams coming off the moors. When I visited, the water cascaded down at the top and then seemed to disappear, with the section under the footbridge being as dry as a bone. I tracked that down to an underground bypass that took the water to the SE corner of Yeoman Hey (the 'culvert detour' on the water plan sketch). Whatever else, the reservoir makers wanted to keep all their options open.

After that it's simple, the path leading alongside the Dove Stone Reservoir and emerging on to the lane at the bottom, where you go right over the incoming Chew Brook, past the boathouse and back to the car.

The lane and brook come down from Chew Reservoir, high up on the moors, and I had aspired to include that in the walk. You can see from the OS maps that you could scale Birchen Clough from the top of Greenfield and then come back south along the Raven, Ashway and Dean edge, before viewing Chew and returning down the lane.

But that was step too far for me. And a step too far for a family walk.

Walk 29 – Holmbridge – Six Reservoirs

A visit to the Digley and Bilberry reservoirs, then via Holme to the Ramsden, Yateholme and Riding Wood reservoirs, and return via Brownhill Reservoir.

Distance and climb	9.1 km (5.7 miles) and 340m (1100 ft), taking about three hours
Grading	Easy to moderate, climbing gradient 1 in 9, children friendly
OS map	Landranger 110
Start	Holmbridge, roadside – try the Broadfield Park estate, off the main road, 250m NE of the church Holmbridge is on the A6024, between the A628 Woodhead Pass and Huddersfield. Parking was limited, but I left my car on the estate without being intrusive. If you drive from Woodhead there is a good view of the area from the Holme Moss car park near the transmitter (marked as a viewpoint on the OS maps)

The walk

From opposite the church, take the track called Digley Road. It's a pleasant wooded walk, with Digley Brook on the left, leading to a set of rusting gates. Go right there, up the steps and through a kissing gate, following the path left and up though the trees to Bank Top Lane. Carry on there to reach the east corner of Digley Reservoir, at the junction with Fieldhead Lane.

In July 2010 the water was very low, well below the overspill. It was built in the 1940s, and they had enough money for the extravagant railed walkway circling the outlet. Why? What function can it have? Having failed to answer that question, walk on

Digley Reservoir overspill

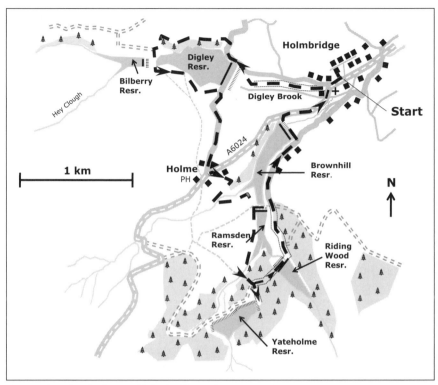

Route Map for Walk 29 – Holmbridge – Six Reservoirs

up the lane (not across the dam) to the right-hand bend, where you can take the kissing gate to avoid further lane walking. The path leads to a track at the top of some steps, where you go left, having first read the useful information boards.

Follow the track by the wooded area alongside the reservoir, avoiding any side paths that go down to the water. There's a set of steps to cross a stream, and within 800m you clear the trees on the left, with a view down to the Bilberry dam. As the main track goes right, take the path down to cross the dam.

Bilberry dam

When you stand in the middle, try jumping up and down. Feels solid enough, doesn't it? If you'd done that in 1852 you'd have been stamping on something that was built by a bunch of cowboys. Imagine the old Bilberry Reservoir at your back, with the Digley Brook leading down the valley to the fore (no Digley Reservoir then, of course). Now think of 25 cm (ten inches) of rain in a week, the overspill system failing to cope, and the dam overtopping. Next come the cracks and the earth slides, and then the whole dam parts at the two ends. It took 30 minutes to empty the reservoir, and within twenty minutes you'd be three miles down the valley, beyond Holmbridge, with the debris from four mills and scores of houses. And you'd be floating alongside 80 other corpses. After that, future dam building in the UK was placed on a much firmer footing.

Having left those thoughts behind you, continue on the other side, following the 'Holmbridge and Holme Walk', through the bilberry bushes that mark the reason for the reservoir's name. In July 2010 the fruit was pitifully small and desiccated. The path keeps close to the reservoir and leads out on to Fieldhead Lane, with another view down to the Digley dam.

Go right there and walk 1 km (half a mile) down to Holme. It's quiet, with a view towards the Holme Moss transmitter. At the main road go left, and then right after 50m, along the public footpath by the 'Underhill' property.

Teletubby garden?

The garden at the rear had a curious 'Teletubbies' design, with domes and caves. I spoke to a man who was mowing, but he could only say, "Dunna ask me lad, I'm newt but gardna." And come what may, the dog would not look at the camera – some animals are like that.

The path goes downhill by a wall, through a gate, continues on the other side of the wall, and then encounters a steep wall stile by the wood before veering right across the pasture. It takes you in a loop over Rake Dike, rising on the other side amongst the trees and veering

Ramsden Reservoir from Brownhill Lane

steadily right, with the first glimpse of Brownhill Reservoir below. Dropping down, you'll reach some railings alongside the path. About 50m before that (the railings are just in view) a path leaves the trees on the right. That will be your onward route, but it's worth having a look at the Ramsden dam first.

At the west end is a channel, with a sluice gate and winding gear. That water does not come off Ramsden Reservoir; it flows from a conduit that runs alongside, from Netherley Clough at the far end. It's a bypass, like some of the other reservoirs visited during these walks, allowing the Water Authority to share the incoming water between the reservoirs according to need.

From the centre of the dam walkway there is a good view below to Brownhill Reservoir, into which all the water from Ramsden flows. I got my best picture of Ramsden from the other side, up on Brownhill Lane, with the brand new spillway, still with its gleaming white concrete.

Returning beyond the railings, follow the path that runs high above the west side of Ramsden, taking you towards Yateholme. It's quite rough, with just the odd decent view, and after 600m the path divides, the right one pointing to the transmitter. Go left, down to the stream, and then turn left on the other side, up to and through the trees. You emerge on to a track near the north corner of Yateholme.

Here there's a difficulty, if you want a photograph. The reservoir is well defended, with earth dams on three sides, and the tracks that circle the water in the forest are not open-access. To get one picture I climbed the gate to the track that goes under the NE side, risking a confrontation with a Ranger, to the east corner. But I'm not advocating it. In fact, I got my best picture from the viewpoint near the transmitter on my way home.

From the north corner, follow the track left (as you reached it from the wood), dropping down across the Riding Wood dam. They were rebuilding at the time, so my

Yateholme Reservoir from Holme Moss viewpoint

freedom of access was limited, and I got no decent picture of Riding Wood. But it was full, like Yateholme, so that was obviously the policy during a drought, keeping a good head.

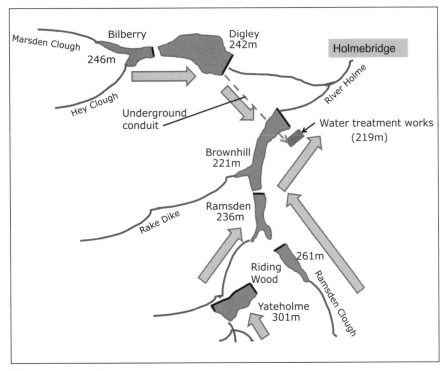

Reservoir flow plan

Turn left from the NE end of Riding Wood dam, following the track and then Brownhill Lane back to the east end of Ramsden dam, and then on alongside Brownhill Reservoir. Now you've see them all, and the sketch shows how the system works, with the flow down to the water treatment works at the east end of the Brownhill dam. It gets there from Digley through an underground conduit. (For these reservoirs, I have not attempted a detailed flow map, with all the conduits and spillways – it was too complex, and the ongoing construction work would soon make it out of date.)

At the Brownhill dam, go left along the public footpath to the NW end, where the path takes you out on to the main road, so you can walk back down into Holmbridge and the car. It's quiet enough, and preferable to the narrow Brownhill Lane on the SE side of the reservoir.

It was at the dam that I met an elderly Yorkshire man, greeting me with, 'Eh up lad, are that alreet? That looks lost.' I was puzzling over the

Brownhill Reservoir and dam

conduit at the NW end, unable to understand why it was running from a half empty reservoir. He was a font of information, as an ex Water Board employee, explaining how it all worked. Many thanks to him! (The conduit is another bypass, as discussed earlier. I reconnoitred this walk before many of the other reservoir walks, and because of that man's insight I was able to better understand how they worked.)

I sneaked a reasonable picture of the dam from the NW end, with the water very low. But when I looked on the Internet, there was a picture showing it full, with the dam wall clearly no longer level with the waterline, having 'settled' at the SE end, by the valve tower. That's a nice word for it! I wonder what the residents of Holmbridge think about it?

Walk 30 – Marsden – Six Reservoirs

Down Mount Road to Butterley Reservoir, on a track to visit the Blakeley and Wessenden reservoirs, around Short Grains Clough and across the moor (Pennine Way) to the Black Moss and Swellands reservoirs. Return is via Redbrook Reservoir. Short Grains Clough presents some hazards, so the walk is best suited for adults and children older than ten. It needs a clear, dry day.

Distance and climb	**9.8 km (6.1 miles) and 340m (1100 ft), taking about 3 hours**
Grading	**Easy, climbing gradient 1 in 14, best for older children**
OS map	**Landranger 110**
Start	**Roadside, by Forest Farm on Mount Road** **From the A63 Oldham to Huddersfield Road, take Mount Road to the east. It's 1 km (half a mile) NE along the main road from the Standedge summit. Forest Farm is then on the left after 1.5 km (a mile), with a golf course to the right**

The walk

Stroll down the lane for 1 km (half a mile), trying to ignore the golfers who are spoiling a good walk, and turn along the public footpath that leaves to the right, 50m after the children's playground. The path takes you past some garages and through the grounds of Bank Top Cottage, to exit through a walker's gate. Go right there (even though the marked right of way goes left down the narrow walled track), then immediately left through another gate. You can then follow that path to the top of the Butterley Reservoir dam. (Butterley means 'good butter pasture'.)

Butterley Reservoir from Blakeley dam

It's a Yorkshire Water reservoir, the last in the chain along the Wessenden valley. When you stand on the dam you can see the outlet for the River Colne at the bottom, and an overspill channel leading to the same spot for when there is high rainfall. Drinking water is taken via an underground pipe, and you'll see the valve-house by the dam that controls the relative flows. Obviously, there has to be a permanent flow for the river to ensure its good health downstream.

On the other side, go right on to Wessenden Road, a wide limestone track, and follow the side of the reservoir up to the next dam, Blakeley (meaning 'dark pasture'). As you approach the top, take the gate on the right so you can walk up to the dam top. It's from there that you get the best view of Butterley Reservoir looking back, and you can visit the valve-house and spillway on the other side. There is no drinking water taken from this; it simply tops up Butterley.

To regain the track, you can go back to the gate or walk along the wall and scale the fence, without damaging it of course. Walking on along Wessenden Road, you get some good views into the valley, and near the top of Blakeley there's an area of higher ground on the right that provides

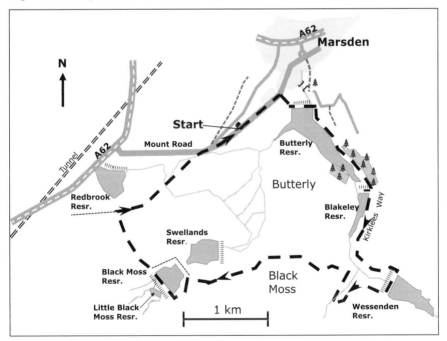

Route Map for Walk 30 – Marsden – Six Reservoirs

good photographic opportunities. You'll pass the Pennine Way marker, pointing down the steep valley. Don't go down there; keep to the track and continue up to the next dam, Wessenden (meaning 'spring'), with a waterfall to admire and, perhaps, some deer to see at the Wessenden Lodge farm.

So Wessenden tops up Blakeley, and further up the valley, outside this walk, Wessenden Head tops up Wessenden. The details are adjacent:

Reservoir	Height above sea level	Capacity Million Litres
Butterley	234m	1800
Blakeley	252m	360
Wessenden	301m	480
Wessenden Head	385m	360

The catchment area of the four reservoirs is 50 times their combined area, similar for other reservoirs covered by these walks. Having crossed the Wessenden dam and the bridge over the weir, go right and follow the path round to Short Grains Clough, with splendid views back down the valley unfolding as you walk. Around the clough there is subsidence, and a steep drop on the right, so caution is needed. You ford the stream at the apex, which is no problem, and there's a waterfall to impress you. Then the path loops back and begins its ascent on to the grass moor. It's paved, because it's the Pennine Way, so it's easy. There's a mast with a solar cell, and a ground bunker. I think it monitors the height of the water table for the water authority.

After 1.5 km (a mile) the next two reservoirs come into view, the path leading to the eastern corner of Black Moss, where there's a notice board with a dramatic story

Blakeley Reservoir – looking north

Wessenden Reservoir – looking east

to read. That reservoir, and Swellands (meaning 'gently undulating moor'), are two of the ten built in the early nineteenth century to provide water for the Huddersfield Narrow Canal, which is 200m below you in the 5 km long Standedge Tunnel.

The sketch shows how it works, with channels taking the water from Swellands to Redbrook and from Black Moss to Brun Clough. That reservoir is by the main road, at the west end of the Standedge cutting. On the OS map you can distinguish the manmade channels from the natural streams because they follow the height contours rather than crossing them steeply downwards.

The sketch gives the heights above sea level (metres), so that the water from Redbrook Reservoir is eventually channelled down Redbrook Clough to top up the Tunnel End reservoir near the point where the canal goes underground. The Brun Clough Reservoir is directly above the tunnel, so

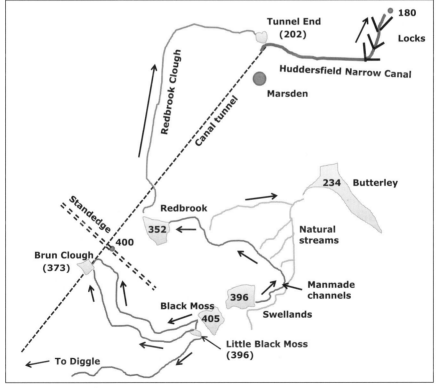

Reservoir water-flow map

there may be a direct shaft from that straight down, I couldn't find out. It's on the wrong side of the Standedge summit to drain to Tunnel End. Beyond Marsden, the canal falls rapidly through many locks, and the same happens at the other end, at Diggle. So, without the top-up reservoirs, the barges going down the locks would quickly empty the tunnel section of its water.

For information regarding the canal and tunnel, including barge trips underground, visit **www.huddersfieldcanal.com**

Rather than follow the path between the reservoirs, I walked along the southern edge of Black Moss, which was easy enough, up to the dam. Standing there, the sun was shining, the wind was blowing, the water was lapping – what more could you want? I got a good picture looking east across the water, with a perfect geological syncline (dished) forming the horizon, outcropping at the two ends (West Nab to the south, Shooters Nab to the north). The sandstone was laid down flat under the sea, then eventually lifted up and, in this case, gently folded. There would have been two reverse folds going on from each end (anticlines – hilled), but they have been long since eroded away, over millions of years.

At the north end of the dam there is a winding device, obviously for opening the sluice, and if you turn round and face west there is a small patch of water 100m away. It is officially a reservoir – Little Black Moss. It's probably the smallest reservoir in the Peak District. Some of the water in Black Moss goes to that, and then on down the hill towards Diggle (where there is another small reservoir, inevitably called Diggle Reservoir), and they appear to top up the Diggle end of the canal.

Walking on, follow the line of the dam NW along the Pennine Way. It's soon paved again, and you cross the county boundary fence before cresting the hill and getting your first view of Redbrook Reservoir. For me, it was a great disappointment, since it was empty, all black mud and forlorn boats beached on the grass. I guess it was under maintenance,

East across Black Moss – Syncline behind

and it explained why Swellands was brimming over, with no water leaving by the channel. (The information board for Redbrook is on the roadside, A62. It's worth stopping off to read it before making for home.)

As you approach the reservoir, the path crosses a gully and intercepts a track, with an old way-marker post. Go right there on the broad grass path – called The Standedge Trail – and follow it back to Mount Road and the car.

Also from Sigma Leisure:

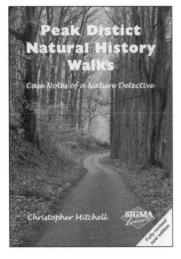

Peak District Walking Natural History Walks
Christopher Mitchell

An updated 2nd Edition with 18 varied walks for all lovers of the great outdoors — and armchair ramblers too! Learn how to be a nature detective, a 'case notes' approach shows you what clues to look for and how to solve them. Detailed maps include animal tracks and signs, landscape features and everything you need for the perfect natural history walk. There are mysteries and puzzles to solve to add more fun for family walks — solutions supplied! Includes follow on material with an extensive Bibliography and 'Taking it Further' sections. *£8.99*

Dark Peak Hikes
Off the Beaten Track
Doug Brown

Here are 30 walks in the Dark Peak - the legendary northern part of the Peak District that covers some of the best hill country of Derbyshire, Yorkshire and Greater Manchester. Renowned for its unique peat ecology and striking gritstone scenery, the Dark Peak is a paradise for adventurous walkers intent on exploring the remoter parts of the moors.

Includes lots of helpful information for each walk – starting point, distance and estimated time, a general description including level of difficulty, and a very detailed route description.
£8.99

All of our books are all available through booksellers. For a free catalogue, please contact:

SIGMA LEISURE, STOBART HOUSE, PONTYCLERC, PENYBANC ROAD AMMANFORD, CARMARTHENSHIRE SA18 3HP
Tel: 01269 593100 Fax: 01269 596116

info@sigmapress.co.uk   www.sigmapress.co.uk